To Harry,
A reminder of happy
Summer days in Englands '67

Gerry.

ON THE
INSPIRATION
OF
SCRIPTURE

ON THE
INSPIRATION
OF
SCRIPTURE

JOHN HENRY NEWMAN

Edited with an Introduction by
J. Derek Holmes and Robert Murray, S.J.

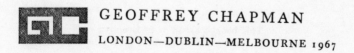

GEOFFREY CHAPMAN

LONDON—DUBLIN—MELBOURNE 1967

Geoffrey Chapman Ltd.,
18 High Street, Wimbledon, London, S.W.19

Geoffrey Chapman (Ireland) Ltd.,
5-7 Main Street, Blackrock, Co. Dublin, Ireland

Geoffrey Chapman Pty. Ltd.,
459 Little Collins Street, Melbourne, Australia

Nihil obstat: R. D. Desmundus Leahy, D.D., Ph.D., L.S.S.,
censor deputatus

Imprimatur: H. Gibney,
Vicarius Generalis

Datum Southwarci die 23a Decembris 1966

This book is set in 11-pt Georgian
Printed in Great Britain by Northumberland Press Limited, Gateshead

CONTENTS

ACKNOWLEDGEMENTS

The editors wish to express their gratitude to the Fathers of the Birmingham Oratory, to the Jesuit Fathers at Farm Street, London, and to the Bishop of Clifton, for permission to use the relevant unpublished material in their respective collections. In particular they wish to thank Father C. Stephen Dessain of the Birmingham Oratory for his valuable help and kind encouragement, to which this book owes its existence. Thanks are also due to Fathers B. Alger and G. MacRae, S.J., and to Mrs Virginia Hastings, who typed the manuscript with most conscientious care.

J. Derek Holmes,
Cambridge.

Robert Murray, S.J.,
Heythrop, 1966.

PART ONE

INTRODUCTION

I THE INSPIRATION OF SCRIPTURE IN NEWMAN'S WRITINGS UP TO 1884

The present volume presents again to the public, after many years of difficult access, the essays on the inspiration of Scripture which John Henry Newman published in 1884 and re-issued, revised, in 1890, in a private edition entitled *Stray Essays*. Newman's thought on Holy Scripture has recently been the subject of a thorough study by Jaak Seynaeve, W.F.,[1] but though he there published some earlier notes of Newman's on inspiration, on the 1884 articles he limited himself to a discussion of their doctrine. Newman's views on inspiration have long been the subject of unfavourable mention in Catholic manuals of theology, and there has been a widespread impression that he was censured by Pope Leo XIII in the encyclical *Providentissimus Deus* of 1893. It is a strange irony that Newman of all men, who both as a man and as a scholar truly lived 'by every word that proceeds from the mouth of God', should have gone down into the manuals as one who held an insufficient view of the inspiration of Scripture. It is to be hoped that since the publication of the *Constitution on Divine Revelation* of Vatican II, Newman will be seen as substantially vindicated in what he was trying to say. But it was admittedly in somewhat bold and unusual language that he said it, and he may have surprised some by his readiness to come to terms with the critics, whenever they were sincere and reverent,

---

[1] *Cardinal Newman's Doctrine on Holy Scripture* (Louvain-Oxford, 1953); more succinct and better digested is Seynaeve's article 'Newman (doctrine scripturaire du Cardinal)', in *Dictionnaire de la Bible*, Supplément, VI (1960), cols. 427-74.

and to speak their language. Since much of this introduction must be concerned with somewhat technical theological discussion, it may be well to begin with a reminder of Newman's lifelong devotion to Scripture as God's word.

On the first page of the *Apologia* Newman tells how he was 'brought up from a child to take great delight in reading the Bible', and throughout his life he valued the 'vast benefit' which comes from the knowledge and reading of Scripture.[1] It was a first principle with him that Scripture must be read with faith, which 'receives with reverence and love whatever God gives'.[2] 'Obedience to God's commandments, which implies knowledge of sin and of holiness, and the desire and endeavour to please Him, this is the only practical interpreter of Scripture doctrine'.[3] A 'plain man' should 'read the Gospels with a serious and humble mind, and as in God's presence';[4] it is man's duty to use the words of Scripture 'humbly, diffidently, and teachably, with the thought of God before us, and of our own nothingness'.[5] Much more did Newman see that scholarly study of Scripture demanded moral as well as intellectual qualities.

> The love of God alone can give such knowledge its right direction. There is the danger lest men so informed find themselves scrutinizing when they should be adoring, reasoning when they should be believing, comparing when they should be choosing, and proving when they should be acting.[6]

Considering the poor Catholics who became his chief

---

[1] Cf. *Grammar of Assent*, pp. 56-7.
[2] *Parochial and Plain Sermons* (PPS) I, p. 211.
[3] Ibid., pp. 54-5.
[4] PPS III, p. 77.
[5] Ibid., p. 369.
[6] PPS VIII, p. 264. Cf. Seynaeve's chapter 'The Ideal of the Christian Exegete' in *Newman's Doctrine*, esp. pp. 363-76.

pastoral concern, Newman grieved at their ignorance of Scripture which cut them off from so great a means of grace:

> It is to them a terra incognita. The Old Testament especially excites no sentiment of love, reverence, devotion or trust. They hear bold things said against it—or fragments of it quoted detached from its context, and they have no associations with it in their affections. It creates in them no distress or horror to hear it contemptuously treated as 'a venerable "book"'.

In a catechism of over three hundred and sixty questions, Newman lamented, there was 'only one poor reference to the Scriptures as a book given by God as a guide and comfort'.[1] It was such pastoral concern for Catholics which prompted the 1884 articles. It is time, however, to turn to the particular subject of this Introduction and to start tracing Newman's theological views on inspiration.

Although he did not consider that the inspiration of Scripture was an intellectual difficulty during many years of his life, Newman's early views on the Bible were never literal or fundamentalist. He always recognized the human element in both the content and form of Scripture. The Bible was not a means of determining physical questions, but was intended for religious purposes. The words of Scripture were imperfect and defective, inspiration being defective, not in itself but because of the medium of human language, the use of human concepts to express divine realities, and because of the persons addressed, namely human beings.[2]

[1] Newman to Monsell, 9 Apr 1883; B(irmingham) O(ratory) A(rchives), P(ersonal) C(orrespondence).
[2] *Fifteen Sermons preached before The University of Oxford* (London, 1906), pp. 59, 268.

Newman's early notions of inspiration were far from defined, but he did not identify it with inerrancy or authenticity. In 1825 he argued against his brother Charles that spuriousness, faultiness or error in the Christian Scriptures did not disprove or discredit the religion of Christianity. He did not consider it was inconsistent to believe that whilst the Canticle of Canticles was wrongly inserted in the Jewish Canon, the Jewish religion was true and its books substantially authentic. To think that certain books were not inspired, or to admit the existence of interpolations and corruptions in the sacred text, was not the same as asserting that a religion was false. The canon of Scripture was fixed by fallible men who could be mistaken. Some critics held that the Apocalypse, the second epistle of St Peter, or even substantial sections of the Gospels were spurious, without denying the truth of the Christian religion. The opinions of these critics might be wrong, but their attitude was not inconsistent, because the New Testament was not Christianity but the record of Christianity. Furthermore, the fact that it was the disciples of apostles, rather than the apostles themselves, who wrote or composed the Gospels from the memory of conversations, did not imply that they could not have had a divine commission. In such a case the books could be substantially true, although with many misstatements which would not invalidate their claim to a divine commission. In any case the apostles themselves might have written them and made mistakes, for they would write as human beings.[1]

Many interesting ideas on the inspiration of Scripture are suggested in Newman's early writings, but there is nothing like a consistent or definitive theory and it would be a mistake to look for one. In 1837 he distinguished between plenary and partial inspiration and thought that only the

[1] 25 Aug 1825; BOA, A4.2.iv.

canonical books were plenarily inspired, while accepting that the Holy Spirit did in fact speak by the apocrypha or deuterocanonical books. The gifts and operations of the Holy Ghost were manifold, allowing of differences of kind and degree.[1] Another example would be the suggestion of the notion of literary forms which Seynaeve sees in Newman's admission in a sermon of 1834 that although Christ's words were sacred and of an abiding force, they were clothed in a temporary garb, served an immediate end, and were difficult to disengage from the temporary and the immediate.[2]

The most significant feature, however, of Newman's ideas on the inspiration of the Bible was his recognition of the human element in the formation and writing of the sacred books. He was prepared to concede that the New Testament was apparently an incomplete document, accidentally preserved, lacking consistency and harmony, and only received as one book in the fourth century. It had no code of commandments or list of fundamentals, but was made up of four lives of Christ, written for different parts of the Church, and which did not make up a whole. Some of the books, such as the epistle to the Laodiceans, were lost. Others, perhaps the Gospel of St Matthew or the epistle to the Hebrews, existed only in translation, while books like the second epistle of St Peter had barely enough evidence for being accepted as genuine.[3]

Later, in 1845, when discussing the antecedent probability of developments in doctrine, Newman pointed out some other limitations of the Scriptures. He showed, for instance, that ideas belonged to a writer and could not be found in a book or a text, even in the case of inspired documents.

[1] *The Via Media* (London, 1901), Vol. II, pp. 179-80.
[2] J. Seynaeve, *Newman's Doctrine*, p. 96; PPS III, pp. 318-19.
[3] *The Via Media*, Vol. I, pp. 281-2.

Nor was it possible for ideas to be conveyed from a writer to a reader immediately, completely or accurately, at first reading. Nor could the sacred writings cover every form which the revelation might assume when submitted to many minds. The mere letter of the Bible could not contain the fulness of revelation; Scripture itself could not solve the questions of canonicity or inspiration; its style was indirect and its structure was unsystematic so that even definitions of the Church depended on obscure sentences.[1]

In *Tract 85* Newman had actually used the human aspect of the inspired writings as an argument in favour of the Church, a destructive or negative *argumentum ad hominem* probably only possible at that particular time, and which Newman himself recognized as dangerous and described as 'a kill-or-cure remedy'.[2] The evidence against Christianity and the Bible was so strong that only the infallible authority of the Church could withstand it; the rejection of the Church system would lead to atheism. The Protestant could not consistently object that the Tractarian believed more than was justified by the Bible without ceasing to believe as much as he did, because the inspiration of Scripture was as difficult to establish from the text of the Bible as the doctrine of apostolic succession.

Whatever might be thought of Newman's argument, it is valuable in the present context because it clearly showed an awareness and acceptance of the difficulties, limitations and the human element in the sacred writings, and this is the point which concerns us here.

In what way inspiration is compatible with that per-

---

[1] *An Essay on the Development of Christian Doctrine* (London, 1906), pp. 55-75.
[2] *Discussions and Arguments on Various Subjects* (London, 1891), p. 112. Cf. also O. Chadwick, *From Bossuet to Newman: The Idea of Doctrinal Development* (Cambridge, 1957), pp. 127-8.

sonal agency on the part of its instruments, which the
composition of the Bible evidences, we know not; but if
anything is certain, it is this,—that, though the Bible is
inspired, and therefore, in one sense, written by God, yet
very large portions of it, if not far the greater part of it,
are written in as free and unconstrained a manner, and
(apparently) with as little apparent consciousness of a
supernatural dictation or restraint, on the part of His
earthly instruments, as if He had had no share in the
work. As God rules the will, yet the will is free,—as He
rules the course of the world, yet men conduct it,—so He
has inspired the Bible, yet men have written it.[1]

Many passages of Scripture would appear at first sight
to most men of the time strange or incredible, superstitious
or extreme, were it not for their reverence for the canon of
Scripture. Newman gave as examples of such passages des-
criptions of a demoniac or finding a coin in a fish's mouth;
events like the visitation, the ascension or the temptation
of Christ; the accounts of Noah and the Ark, Jonah in the
whale, and Abraham or Isaac denying their wives. Scripture
could also be misleading; in the New Testament, the proxi-
mity of the Parousia was suggested, little was said about
post-baptismal sin and the Synoptics implied the subordina-
tion of the Son; in the Old Testament, the Canticle did not
hint at a spiritual meaning, while the first meaning of the
prophecy of Immanuel, 'a Virgin shall conceive', did not
refer to Christ but to an event of the day.

Scripture was not always consistent; there were two
stories of creation in Genesis, it was difficult to reconcile
the different accounts of the Resurrection, and there were
two discrepant accounts of the death of Judas. The picture
given of David in Chronicles and the Psalms did not seem

---

[1] *Discussions and Arguments*, pp. 145-6.

to be the same as that given in the Books of Samuel. The text of the Sermon on the Mount in Luke seemed a corrupt version of that found in Matthew. Some parallels, such as the miracles of Elijah and Elisha, might be suspected, while the feeding of the four and five thousand would seem to be two different accounts of the same event. The tone of Romans was not the same as that of Hebrews, Deuteronomy appeared to contradict Exodus, and the Synoptics seemed to contradict the Gospel of St John.

Newman maintained in the course of his argument that Scripture was as obscure, indirect and even conflicting in relating the facts of the sacred history as in stating sacred doctrine. The narrative in both cases was written in a free, natural and unsystematic manner without attempting to be either complete or consistent. Events were alluded to instead of being fully reported. The structure of Scripture was not regular or methodical, its communications were unsystematic and uncertain, and the writings themselves were collected as if casually or accidentally. The Bible had all the characteristics of an uninspired book. It was possible to speak of the intentions of a particular writer who was influenced by certain circumstances, who omitted, introduced or supplied when dealing with his material and who took pains over his work or left it incomplete. The writing would have the characteristics of the time, place, person or character involved, with traces of dialect and style, while the same events would be reported differently by different writers.

Throughout his argument Newman never ignored his main point, that since the writing was irregular, inconsistent or incomplete, it was antecedently highly improbable that it would contain the whole of the revealed Word of God. The Bible did not contain a complete secular history, and there was no reason why it should contain a

complete account of religious truth. It was unreasonable
to demand an adequate scriptural foundation for Church
doctrines, if the impression gained from the Bible was of
writers who took solemn and sacred truths for granted
and who did not give a complete or full treatment of the
sense of revelation. The writings did not reflect all the
beliefs of the writer and events were often presented without comment or moral implication. Scripture did not interpret itself, often startling facts were narrated simply,
needing the understanding of the Church, and even essential truths were not made clear. There was no mention, for
example, of the apostles being baptized, but this could be
paralleled by other omissions such as the healing of Mal-
chus' ear in St John, a defective account which Protestants
would call unnatural if it were a matter of doctrine and
not a question of history.

Newman claimed that the objections brought against the
Catholic system were paralleled by those which could be
brought against the canon of Scripture. It was possible to
take exception to many things in Scripture which were
believed by those who rejected Catholic doctrines, but the
canon of Scripture and Catholic doctrines rested on the
same foundation, and those who disputed the latter should
also question the former. Patristic or scriptural evidence was
lacking, not only for Catholic doctrines but also for the
canonicity, authority or inspiration of Scripture itself. The
Book of Esther was not quoted in the New Testament, was
rejected by Melito and Gregory Nazianzen, contained no
prophecy or sign of being a religious history, and was of a
very startling character. To some extent, similar remarks
might be made about Ecclesiastes or the Canticles, while
other plausible arguments could be found against the
Apocalypse, the second epistle of St Peter, or those of St
James and St Jude. Church doctrines might only be ob-

scurely gathered from Scripture, but Scripture was only obscurely gathered from history.

It was impossible to accept the canon of Scripture without the authority of the ancient Church; the Bible and the Catholic system went together and the denial of one would lead to the denial of the other. The internal evidence of Scripture was inadequate for, or even contrary to, the idea of inspiration. It was impossible to believe in the infallibility of the Bible without accepting the infallibility of the ancient Church which also taught other, Catholic, doctrines. Revelation of its very nature must be plain to all, but revelation was not plainly in Scripture alone, but in the exposition of the Church and explanations of the Fathers.

Speaking of some doctrinal passages in Scripture, Newman commented:

> . . . these and a multitude of other passages would be adduced, not to prove that Christianity was not true, or that Christ was not the Son of God, or the Bible not inspired, or not on *the whole* genuine and authentic, but that every part of it was not *equally* divine; that portions, books, particularly of the Old Testament, were not so; that we must use our own judgment. Nay, as time went on, perhaps it would be said that the Old Testament altogether was not inspired, only the New—nay, perhaps only parts of the New, not certain books which were for a time doubted in some ancient Churches, or not the Gospels according to St Mark and St Luke, nor the Acts, because not the writing of Apostles, or not St Paul's reasonings, only his conclusions. Next, it would be said, that no reliance can safely be placed on single texts; and so men would proceed, giving up first one thing, then another, till it would become a question what they gained of any kind, what they considered they gained, from

Christianity as a definite revelation or a direct benefit. They would come to consider its publication mainly as an historical event occurring eighteen hundred years since, which modified or altered the course of human thought and society, and thereby altered what would otherwise have been our state; as something infused into an existing mass, and influencing us in the improved tone of the institutions in which we find ourselves, rather than as independent, substantive, and one, specially divine in its origin, and directly acting upon us.[1]

The denial of the Church as a divine institution would be followed by a denial of the existence of any Christian system, doctrine or creed, and the Bible would be given up as well as the Church. It was a man's duty to believe the whole of revelation because God had given a revelation. The whole of Scripture should be accepted and all Church doctrines, whether it was possible to prove that a particular part of Scripture was genuine or not, or completely prove all the doctrines of the Church.

Whether I can prove this or that part to my satisfaction, yet, since I can prove all in a certain way, and cannot separate part from part satisfactorily, I cannot be wrong in taking the whole. I am sure that, if there be error, which I have yet to learn, it must be, not in principles, but in mere matters of detail. If there be corruption or human addition in what comes to me, it must be in little matters, not in great. On the whole, I cannot but have God's Revelation, and that, in what I see before me, with whatever incidental errors.[2]

It would obviously be false to see *Tract 85* either as a

[1] Ibid., pp. 231-2.
[2] Ibid., p. 234.

simple acceptance of the findings of scientific criticism, or as a clear and consistent description of Newman's attitude towards the inspiration of Scripture. Newman tended to be vague in his use of the word 'inspiration' and did not really define the sense of it in connection with the many critical points which he instanced. He would seem to have considered that errors were only possible in matters of detail, and whatever he said about the results of criticism was apparently qualified by his belief in 'inspiration', but he did not discuss this point. Newman in fact was not dealing with a problem of Scripture but with an argument in favour of the Church. At the same time, when *Tract 85* is considered beside other remarks he had made elsewhere, particularly in the paper written in 1825, it is clear that he not only admitted the human element in the Bible, but accepted the possibility of distinguishing between the results of biblical criticism and the truth of the Christian religion. He had therefore already made the distinctions which would enable him to accept the findings of criticism without difficulty.

One of the reasons why Newman had no difficulty in accepting the human element in the Bible was his appreciation of the Fathers, whose ideas on Scripture and inspiration could often be far more 'liberal' than those of later theologians. Another important factor was his recognition that 'what is historically human may be doctrinally divine'.[1] Christianity, according to Newman, had two aspects, one external or human, and the other internal or divine. These were not two facts but two aspects of one integral whole, and to deal with one without the other was unreal, sophisti-

---

[1] From a paper (A.11.2, p. 9) dating from the Anglican period, possibly from 1836, and published by Seynaeve, *Newman's Doctrine*, p. 31*. This point was the burden of Newman's critique, published in 1841, of Dean Milman's *History of Christianity:* cf. *Essays Critical and Historical* (London, 1919), Vol. II, pp. 186-248, matter from which is summarized in this paragraph of our text.

cal and extravagant. The existence, for example, of pagan parallels to Christian doctrines or practices was not an argument against Christianity, but confused an external appearance with an internal reality. He admitted, for instance, the resemblance between the Magianism of the East and Judaism after the Captivity, and that the Magnificat was essentially Jewish. He did not object to the association of John the Baptist with the Essenes, nor to the parallels between Christian and Oriental asceticism. Resemblances between Christian beliefs and the ideas of pagan philosophers, did not conflict with the possibility of a supernatural cause or the existence of a divine revelation.

A further significant factor was that, as an Anglican and as a Catholic, Newman accepted the importance of the Church and Tradition as means of revelation. Newman, it must be emphasized, held a 'one-source theory' of revelation. He believed that the Church and Tradition taught the truth, while Scripture verified, vindicated or proved that teaching. The Bible and Tradition made up the joint rule of faith, antiquity strengthened the faint but real intimations of doctrine given in Scripture, the Bible was interpreted by Tradition which was verified by Scripture.[1] Although written by inspired men, the Bible was never intended to teach doctrine to the majority of Christians, but was written for those already instructed in doctrine. The writings of Scripture, teaching for instance by intimation or implication, demanded such qualities for understanding its teaching that the prudent man would use the help of any subsidiary guides. The qualifications necessary, however, could best be found in the collective Church, which might 'be truly said almost infallibly to interpret

[1] *The Via Media*, Vol. I, pp. 29, 274; *The Arians of the Fourth Century* (London, 1901), p. 50. Cf. the Letter to Pusey, *Difficulties of Anglicans*, Vol. II, pp. 11-13.

Scripture aright'. It might be possible for an individual Christian to gain the whole truth from the Bible, but the chances were 'very seriously against a given individual' doing so in practice.[1]

When still an Anglican, Newman had once expressed the fear that only the Roman Church could withstand the 'league of evil' forming against the Bible.[2] When he became a Catholic and his religion became less dependent on the Bible, he felt that he too could withstand it more easily, and for many years he had no difficulties with the question of inspiration. In 1866 he argued that Catholics received the canon of Scripture on the authority of the Church and that it was easier to show the authority of the Church than that of the Bible. He followed St Augustine in admitting that he would not believe in the Gospel, if he had not been moved by the authority of the Catholic Church.[3] In the *Apologia*, while accepting that Scripture was divine, he questioned whether it could maintain religious truth in an anarchical world. He himself believed that experience proved that the Bible could not answer this purpose, for which indeed it had never been intended. A book could not 'make a stand against the wild living intellect of man'.[4] Revelation could not be preserved by a book but needed an infallible authority.

Newman still continued to recognize the human aspect of the inspired writings. In a university lecture given in November 1858 he made a distinction between Literature, which was of a personal character and dealt with ideas, and Science, which dealt with realities and discussed what was universal and eternal. As Scripture excluded the personal

[1] *The Via Media*, Vol. I, pp. 138-43, 157-9.
[2] *Letters and Correspondence of John Henry Newman*, ed. Anne Mozley (London, 1891), Vol. II, p. 300.
[3] *Discussions and Arguments*, p. 366.
[4] *Apologia pro vita sua* (London, 1905), p. 245.

elements of the writer and rose to the region of 'pure and
mere inspiration', when it ceased in any sense to be the
writing of a man, it belonged to the realm of *Science* and
not *Literature*. At such times the Bible conveyed heavenly
truths, unseen verities and divine manifestations alone, and
not the ideas or feelings of the human instrument, who did
not cease to be a man although inspired or infallible. The
epistles of St Paul, for instance, were really and truly personal and so *Literature*, because although they revealed
objective truth, they were also subjective. Other parts of the
Bible, such as the beginning of St John's Gospel, were of the
nature of *Science* and merely enunciated eternal things,
'without (so to say) the medium of any human mind trans-
mitting them to us'.[1] In such a passage, Newman would
seem to envisage the possibility of 'degrees' of inspiration
or a 'qualitative' significance of the sacred writings as the
Revealed Word of God.

When *Essays and Reviews* was published in 1860 and the
question of plenary inspiration was a burning issue, Newman considered that it was a problem which belonged
exclusively to Protestantism. Catholics received the whole
Bible as the Word of God on the authority of the Church,
which had defined very little

as to the aspects under which it comes from God, and the
limits of its inspiration. Supposing for argument sake
that it could be proved that some passage in the Pentateuch about Egyptian History were erroneous, nay, let
the universality of the Deluge over the globe, or the
literal interpretation be for argument sake disproved, it
would not affect a Catholic, for two reasons: (1) Because
the Church has not made these points *de fide*, and (2)
because, not the Bible, but the Church, is to him the

[1] *The Idea of a University* (London, 1905), pp. 289-90.

oracle and organ of Revelation; so that, though the whole
Scripture were miraculously removed from the world as
if it had never been, evil and miserable as would be the
absence of such a privilege, he would still have motives
and objects for his faith. Whereas, to the Protestant, the
question is one of life and death.[1]

Nevertheless, in 1861 and again in 1863, Newman was
working on the theological problem of inspiration. His
notes, the total compass of which suggests that he intended
a more exhaustive treatment than he was to give in the
articles of 1884, were published by J. Seynaeve in 1953.[2]
Though Newman had planned an introduction, to be called
'Prolegomena', to the Bible translation which in 1857 Wise-
man had invited him to undertake, the notes of 1861-3
appear to be quite distinct from his draft for the 'Prolegomena' (which in any case he is thought to have destroyed
in 1877).[3] The latter was to have been an apologetic work,
whereas the extant notes, though they evince the same concern as inspired the articles of 1884, to show what Catholics
may or must hold about Scripture in face of contemporary
criticism and scientific thought, are rather a meditative
inquiry. Dating as they do from Newman's period of greatest depression and suffering, the notes represent two
attempts, both abandoned, to discuss the problems of biblical inspiration, its nature, scope and extent. The notes are
important as showing that many of the characteristic ideas
in the 1884 articles had been in gestation not merely, as
Newman said in answer to Healy, for 'about a twelvemonth',
but for at least twelve years. Reference will be made below

[1] Newman to Malcolm MacColl, 24 Mar 1861; reprinted in *The
Observer*, 8 Sep 1929, p. 11, where it is wrongly stated to have been
addressed to Sir Andrew Clark.

[2] In *Newman's Doctrine*, pp. 60*-144*.

[3] W. Ward, *Life* I, pp. 417-28; Seynaeve, *Newman's Doctrine*, p. 57*.

to passages in these notes which illustrate the 1884 articles: they cannot be summarized conveniently here, because of their disordered and provisional character.[1] In place of such an attempt we may refer to other evidence of Newman's ideas on biblical inspiration at this time, from letters and memoranda, some of them not yet published, which offer parallels to the notes of 1861-3. All give the impression that, in this period before the first Vatican Council defined the notion of inspiration more precisely than had previously been done, and thereby seemed to take a position more in conflict with the findings of criticism, Newman did not consider that the inspiration of Scripture posed any special problem for Catholics. In 1864 he pointed out that little had been defined by the Church on inspiration and thought it highly unlikely that the freedom which Catholics then enjoyed would be restricted in any way. The Church had never determined, for example, that the words of the Bible should be understood in a literal sense, and therefore the fact that the earth moved did not mean that Scripture was untrue. Although theologians did not admit error in the Bible, they would have to allow that statements such as the sun 'rising', were in accordance with popular ideas and that the writers of Scripture were not guaranteeing the fact but expressing an historical opinion. Newman also thought that the teaching of theologians, which in any case was not infallible, would also allow a Catholic to hold that Moses

[1] The student is directed to Seynaeve's work, but with a warning: not only is the transcription unreliable, but also the editor, in his zeal to reconstruct what he regards as an unknown book by Newman (for which he has composed a title and sub-headings), seems to have missed the extent to which the notes are a record of dialectical thinking, not yet brought to a conclusion. E.g. on p. 121* he transcribes 'The former . . . is incapable of subdivision . . .', but he has missed another note written on the same day, in which Newman says 'Each of these antagonist views admit of subdivision' (A.23.1, under which both documents are now catalogued). This is, unfortunately, far from being the only inaccuracy in Seynaeve's transcription.

merely assembled pre-existing documents or even that he
was only associated in some way with the writings
concerned. He also considered that a Catholic was not
bound to the literal sense of the first chapter of Genesis,
nor to accept the Davidic authorship of the Psalms.

At the same time, however, Catholics were under the
obligation of not giving scandal. They should be unwilling
to surrender received opinions about inspiration in the case
of existing but uncertain scientific inquiries indirectly bearing on Scripture, until they were proved untenable, by
which time men would be prepared to change.[1] Meanwhile
all that had been defined on the subject of inspiration was
that God was the 'author' of both Old and New Testaments,
that is covenants or dispensations, not that he was the
writer of the books of Scripture. Newman claimed that
there was no dogmatic assertion of the inspiration of Scripture, although it was defined that the writers were inspired.
He also thought that inspiration extended only to faith
and morals, and that in secular fields such as politics or
physics, the most that Catholics believed was that Scripture
was not wrong, not that it was right.[2]

Newman's opinions were often given to correspondents
in private letters or memoranda, and these were sometimes
published. In one such memorandum he repeated his claim

[1] This is a quite different point from Newman's insistence in the
1861-3 papers that Catholics should not hold on to discredited positions
and only finally surrender them when they were absolutely disproved.
Newman is here speaking of the danger of scandal and the majority of
uneducated men, not of the need for academic freedom and the rights
of the intellectual minority. Furthermore Newman in the present context was speaking of uncertain inquiries only indirectly bearing on
Scripture and warning against the temptation of falling for the latest
scientific opinion.

[2] Newman to Wordsworth, 22 Oct 1864; BOA, M(iscellaneous)
L(etters); there is also a copy in V(arious) C(ollections), 11. Newman had
made a careful study of the phrase 'auctor utriusque testamenti' in the
1861-3 papers; see Seynaeve, *Newman's Doctrine*, pp. 76*-84*, and Part
III of this Introduction.

that the Church had determined very little on the subject
of the authority of Scripture and had not formally defined
that Scripture was inspired.[1] What had been defined was
that God was *auctor utriusque Testamenti*, but not that he
was *auctor omnium librorum* which belonged to each Testament. Catholics, however, were not at liberty to deny at
once the inspiration of Scripture, because of the words of
St Paul, the opinion of the early Fathers, the universal feeling of the Church and the consent of all the theologians.
The inspiration of Scripture might not be *de fide* but it was
the duty of Catholics not to encourage, spread or defend
doubts about it.

With regard to the extent of inspiration, Newman did
not think that the Council of Trent had spoken of it as the
authoritative channel of doctrine in matters other than
faith and morals, but that the difficult task of trying to state
distinctly what pertained to faith and morals in the text
of Scripture was not one which could be left to individuals.
While eventually it became clear that faith and morals were
not involved in a doctrine apparently taught in Scripture—
that the sun moved round the earth—time was needed to
ascertain the fact that the earth did move, and therefore
that the Holy Spirit did not dictate those expressions in
Scripture which implied that it did not, or rather that there
was no intention of conveying that notion by those
expressions.

Dealing with more specific questions, Newman wrote that
he did not see anything in Scripture which obliged or even
led to the six days of Genesis being considered as literal

[1] C. Kegan Paul, 'John Henry, Cardinal Newman', in *The Century
Illustrated Monthly Magazine*, Vol. XXIV (New Series, Vol. II, 1882),
pp. 273-86. The passage on inspiration was reprinted in *The Weekly
Register*, Vol. 65, No. 1691 (Saturday, June 3, 1882), pp. 673-4. In spite
of the late date of publication, the content of the memorandum and
absence of any mention of the Vatican Council would suggest that it
was written before the Council.

days. The literal accuracy of the histories of Jonah or Elisha rested on a different principle, that of the possibility of miracles and whether they should be expected. On the personal level, Newman had no difficulty in believing that on a particular occasion, iron was as light as wood, if it was God's will to work miracles or act contrary to general experience. While he would say the same about Jonah and the whale, he did feel 'the additional grave and awful hazard how to attempt to deny the history without irreverence toward the express teaching of the incarnate God'.[1] He was, then, prepared to allow that the stories of Jonah and Elisha might not be historical although he himself found it difficult to deny the historicity of Jonah, and had no personal difficulty in believing the miracles of Elisha.

There was a real link in Newman's mind between the notions and limitations of inspiration and infallibility. He once wrote that he wished to hold 'that the Church never will be able to answer, or has been able to answer, what the Apostles could not answer, e.g. whether the earth is stationary or not, or whether a republic is or is not better than a monarchy'.[2] This in fact was the line of thought which Newman adopted and even if at times he failed to make a sharp distinction between inspiration and inerrancy, he was able to say of St Paul, 'He was not promised inerrancy as regards his notions or his statements about the motion of the heavenly bodies. There were things he did know, and things he did not know.' In the same way, he went on, although the task of the Church was to resolve the difficulties of revelation and preach the doctrine to be believed, she was unable to answer many questions

[1] *The Weekly Register*, p. 674. Newman means that the natural sense of Mt. 12:40 suggests that Jesus regarded the story as historical.
[2] BOA, A.43.12, 15 Feb 1868. Reprinted by C. S. Dessain in *The Journal of Theological Studies*, New Series, IX (1958), p. 333.

because she did not know more than the apostles knew.[1]

Inspiration and infallibility were also linked in Newman's mind by the definitions of the Vatican Council:

> The two main instruments of infidelity just now are physical science and history; physical science is used against Scripture, and history against dogma; the Vatican Council by its decrees about the Inspiration of Scripture and the Infallibility of the Pope has simply thrown down the gauntlet to the science and historical research of the day.[2]

It was not that Newman had any personal difficulty in accepting the canons of the Council on inspiration, but he felt they had been drawn up and passed without sufficient attention being paid to contemporary criticism. Theologians had not sufficiently anticipated some of the difficulties which the definitions would raise, and the subsequent need for a theological explanation and interpretation of the canons which would be different, in some respects, from what appeared to be their *prima facie* sense.

He had learned that the definitions were not intended to make certain theological opinions untenable, but this had apparently not been taken into account in the wording adopted. Had the discussion been more free and open, the Council would have been able to avoid such mistakes; but the Pope and the bishops appeared, he said, to have left everything to the Holy Spirit. Full deliberation was necessary, not for the validity of the decrees, but in order to satisfy the responsibilities of those who had passed them, and on such important matters all sides should be considered and reviewed. As it was, the definitions of the

---

[1] Newman to Hutton, 20 Oct 1871; BOA, P(ersonal) C(orrespondence), copy.

[2] Quoted in W. Ward, *The Life of John Henry Cardinal Newman* (London, 1912), Vol. II, pp. 311-12.

Council led to the questions whether it was compatible with 'inspiration' to hold that Moses selected and put together pre-existing documents, for example, or whether all the genealogies were 'inspired'.[1]

According to Newman, 'the Vatican Council has quite superseded the Tridentine, in the question of Inspiration'. It had done this by defining that books were inspired and not only the writers, and that *de fide*; God was declared the author of the books of Scripture and not simply indirectly as the author of the Testaments, covenants or dispensations.[2] But he also felt that the Vatican Council had not altered the fact 'that the issue of inspiration is for docrine and morals'.[3] Although Newman felt that the Council had restricted the freedom which Catholics had previously enjoyed, he had no intention of fideistically rejecting scientific conclusions or historical facts. The new definition given to the theological notion of inspiration would have to be reconciled with the findings of criticism.

The main question centred on the meaning of 'inspiration'; 'However, the question returns—the 4th Book of Kings (or Paralipomenon) I think, speaks of an army of a million men—are such statements inspired?'[4] Two years later, Newman referred to an article by Professor Owen which scientifically discussed the limits of the age of man and the evidence for the Patriarchs being essentially the same type of human being as contemporary man;

I wish some of your theologians would look at it in the

---

[1] Ibid., pp. 293-5.

[2] Newman, of course, later modified this and did not believe that the Council had prevented an understanding of inspiration based on this distinction.

[3] Newman to Penny, 20 May 1878; VC 11; there is also a copy in C(opied) L(etters).

[4] Newman to Coleridge, 9 Jun 1870; PC copy, autograph Farm St. This letter was written to the same correspondent two days after that quoted in Ward, *Life* II, pp. 294-5.

light of the definition of 1870 about Scripture. I trust we ιδιῶται have a right to claim instruction from those who took part in the Council, what we are to say, after reading it, about V.Ch: of Genesis—Are we to say that the lengths of the lives of the Patriarchs were *miraculous* or *natural*? And in what part of the world were they?[1]

Newman complained that many theologians decided questions about Scripture which the Church had not decided, and that the Vatican Council had defined points which had previously been open questions, without pronouncing questions open which many writers were determined to close.[2] He therefore placed great stress on the need to open the question, or treat it as open. Clifford's explanation of the days of creation and the subsequent controversy was an example of the type of discussion which Newman felt was essential. The Bishop believed that the first 34 verses of Genesis were a sacred hymn consecrating each day of twenty-four hours in the week to the memory of the works of the Creator. Other Catholics preferred to defend Genesis 1 as historical by interpreting 'days' as periods of time, attempting to reconcile Genesis with scientific findings and even claiming that scientific information might be revealed by God if it were necessary. Newman wrote to Clifford:

It rejoices me to see in the Dublin the account given of the criticisms passed on your late Article on Gen. i. It shows you have succeeded in opening the door, tho' the critics do not like the particular way in which you have opened it. They seem all to imply, some avow, that you *have* opened it. We need not seek to shake ourselves free

[1] Newman to Coleridge, 1 Mar 1872; PC copy. 'V.Ch:', Genesis ch. 5. Cf. R. Owen, 'On Longevity', in *Frazer's Magazine*, New Series, V (1872), pp. 218-33.
[2] Newman to Lord Emly, 9 Apr 1883; PC.

from science any longer, since you have suggested an interpretation which ignores science altogether.[1]

The primary aim of Newman's article 'On the Inspiration of Scripture' was to show that it was not a closed question, and to ease the consciences of intellectual Catholics by showing that the legitimate instruments of criticism could be used. Newman was certainly anxious about the problem of inspiration and the relation of science and dogma, but he also felt that if the Holy See, which always acted with great deliberation, had not made a decision on a certain point, it might have decided by that very silence to leave certain questions open.[2] He could therefore maintain that the rigidly literalist and fundamentalist outlook which identified inspiration with inerrancy, was not the official teaching of the Catholic Church. There was no need to defend the scientific and historical statements found in the Bible, without asking what type of history was recorded in Scripture or what were the intentions of the human author.

W. E. Addis, who had been consulted by Newman before the 'Note' was published, tried to persuade Ignatius Ryder to 'see more good in the Cardinal's essay than you seem to do'. Addis agreed with some of Ryder's criticisms, such as that the statement that Nabuchodonosor was King of Nineveh expressed the deliberate conviction of a writer who professed to be historical, and was by no means said '*obiter*'. On the other hand, he felt that there was some authority for supposing that the writers of Scripture might

[1] Newman to Clifford, 20 Jan 1883; Clifton. Cf. W. Clifford, 'The Days of the Week, and the Works of Creation', in *The Dublin Review*, Third Series, V (1881), pp. 311-32; 'The Days of Creation: A Reply', ibid., VI (1881), pp. 498-507; J. S. Vaughan, 'Bishop Clifford's Theory of the Days of Creation', ibid., IX (1883), pp. 32-47. See also this Introduction, III, pp. 77-8.

[2] W. Ward, *Life*, Vol. II, p. 505, footnote.

err *'de minimis'*. 'But what I do most strongly feel is this—
that a large part of the O.T. is now laid open to intelligent
criticism.' To claim that Solomon was the author of Ecclesiastes would be to deny that the Hebrew tongue had any
history, and to maintain the unity of authorship of Isaiah
and Zechariah would make real exegesis and criticism
impossible.

But e.g. Law told Dean Stanley that these questions were
absolutely closed to a Catholic and I should have been
afraid to to (sic) publish my conviction. Now the Cardinal
has made all this safe and probable. Were I to get into
trouble with my Bishop, I should simply appeal to the
Cardinal's essay—And I for one am most grateful to
him. It is a practical advantage to me. Law wrote to me
the other day, saying that many would be similarly
thankful.

Addis was the type of Catholic for whom Newman was
probably writing. He did not look to Newman's essay for a
solution of his problems and in fact claimed that as far as
he could see no theory possible to a Catholic would meet all
his difficulties about the Bible, which were never likely to
be answered. At the same time, Addis had no temptation to
adopt the 'infidel' view of the Bible which in any case he
could not even understand, because he was convinced that
it contained in the most strict and exclusive sense God's
revelation, and he could never be unhappy while he had the
strength to read it. But Newman's article admitted the
validity of scientific criticism and recognized that the question of inspiration was far from being closed, and for this
Addis was profoundly grateful. Indeed he spoke of having
tried to make a 'dash for freedom' himself, in an article on
the Vulgate.[1]

[1] Addis to Ryder, 9 Feb 1884; VC 205.

B

II THE ARTICLES OF 1884, THEIR GENESIS
AND THEIR RECEPTION

The article 'On the Inspiration of Scripture', which appeared in *The Nineteenth Century* and was later published as the first of the *Stray Essays*, was apparently a reply to an article said to be called 'History, Criticism and the Roman Catholic Church', which commented on the English edition, just published, of Ernest Renan's *Recollections of my Youth*.[1] Newman's article was originally printed in the form of a pamphlet and sent to several readers for their comments. By comparing the notes, drafts and proofs of this article and the answer to Healy, and by examining Newman's correspondence, it is possible to trace the changes which he made in the two essays and the reasons which prompted him.

Bishop William Clifford of Clifton was one of those whose advice Newman sought. He asked him, for example, whether it was necessary to hold that Solomon wrote Ecclesiastes, and commented 'I believe we are not bound to consider that St Paul wrote the Epistle to the Hebrews, though of course the writer, whoever he was, was inspired'.[2]

[1] Neither Fr Seynaeve (cf. *Newman's Doctrine*, pp. 77-8, n. 2) nor the present editors have succeeded in tracing the article in question, which Miss Meriol Trevor (*Newman: Light in Winter*, p. 605) mistakenly states to have appeared in *The Nineteenth Century*. Newman's reference to it (Essay I, § 2) shows that it was commenting on the recent appearance of Renan's *Souvenirs d'enfance et de jeunesse* (Paris, 1883), in the English version (*Recollections of my youth*, London, 1883). The basis for comment in the sense quoted by Newman can be found in *Recollections* . . . , pp. 255-64.

[2] Newman to Clifford, 7 Jan 1883; Clifton.

It is possible, however, to exaggerate the help which Newman received. While he received more help from Clifford
than anyone else, this assistance was often marginal and
Clifford tended to qualify any admissions which he made.
He conceded, for instance, that St Paul did not write the
epistle to the Hebrews; Catholic writers had adopted the
view that it was written by Luke or Barnabas and adopted
and circulated by Paul, but he also admitted that other
Catholics differed from this view and had not, to his knowledge, been censured. At the same time Clifford was helpful.
He recommended several books and writers, including
Patrizi, who was used by Newman in his essay, and he
pointed out that 'the *verbal* inspiration of Scripture, is held
at the present day by very few catholic divines'.[1]

When Newman was making the point, in his pamphlet,
that a book could be inspired even though not a word of it
was original, he distinctly stated that 'such is the case of
St Matthew's Gospel'.[2] He discussed the lost Hebrew
original and the Greek translation, and maintained that the
translator was also inspired. He also asserted categorically
that 'The Book of Ecclesiasticus is another instance',[3] of a
simple translation which was inspired, not because the
original compiler, but because the translator was inspired.
Here Newman was attempting to reconcile a theory of inspiration with the findings of scientific criticism, and it is
significant that he was perfectly willing to use an example
from the New Testament, as well as the Old. In *Stray
Essays*, however, these examples were replaced by a far
more tentative or qualified one, and Newman did not discuss the example himself but simply quoted from another
writer.

[1] Clifford to Newman, 9 Jan 1883; BOA, VC 21.
[2] § 23.
[3] Ibid.

Clifford and Bishop Hedley objected to the passage about Matthew on the grounds that a translator was not inspired, because language and composition belonged to the author and did not form an essential element of the inspiration of the book. A translation could be as truly the inspired word of God as the original, if it fully expressed the meaning of the original. It was not necessary that the translator or the translations should be inspired. At the same time, neither Clifford nor Hedley considered any of Newman's statements open to censure.[1]

While Newman was not sure that he had quite understood this objection, he emended the passage, leaving out the greater part of it, and expressed his willingness to leave out the whole paragraph because he did not want to say anything novel.[2] Clifford therefore clarified his meaning and explained that since Newman was arguing that a book might be inspired even if the *matter* was not original, as in the case of the Second Book of Maccabees, the example of St Matthew, which was concerned with the original *language*, was not really suitable. Newman's example implied that the language was inspired, whereas it was the matter which was inspired because St Matthew was inspired. A translation had to be authentic, not inspired; the inspiration of the original covered the translation. This also applied to Newman's other example, that of Ecclesiasticus.[3] Newman had no doubt that the passage in question should be omitted, because he thought it would never do to throw down a debatable proposition for discussion. His own opinion was that Scripture might have more than one sense and a text more than one meaning, which one language might admit but which a translation might not preserve.

[1] Clifford to Newman, 20 Sep 1883; VC 21.
[2] Newman to Clifford, 25 Sep 1883; Clifton.
[3] Clifford to Newman, 30 Sep 1883; VC 21.

Since he was not concerned with the senses of Scripture in the pamphlet, he felt he could omit the passage about St Matthew without any difficulty.[1]

Another point, however, might be made. Newman seems to have recognized the composite character of Genesis and the Gospels,[2] and it is clear from the context of his essay[3] that he wished to restrict the notion of 'inspiration' to the final form of the work, excluding original extrinsic sources as not necessarily 'inspired'. Furthermore, if he intended to write an essay on inspiration which left open as much of the question as possible—and his care to avoid being categorical or definitive on any position he adopted would seem to indicate this—then Clifford's correction would mark a limitation which Newman had originally not intended. It would seem that Newman did not set out to 'solve' the question of inspiration or give a final or definitive view, but that he meant to show that the question was still an open one.

Archbishop Errington thought that there was a flaw in the substance of Newman's argument, and also complained of six accidental expressions, although he admitted that these contained 'nothing of much moment'. The drift of Newman's argument, according to the Archbishop, especially in the last paragraph of section 4 and those of 5 and 6, seemed to suppose that there was no sin against faith, although there might be against charity, except in maintaining opinions which were opposed to formal definitions of the Church as being heretical. Errington thought that opinions which had been condemned under any of the other theological terms which might be used, could not be maintained without sinning against faith. Formal definitions of Popes and Councils were not the only rule of faith,

[1] Newman to Clifford, 3 Oct 1883; Clifton.
[2] Cf. R. E. Prothero and G. G. Bradley, *The Life and Correspondence of Arthur Penrhyn Stanley, D.D.* (London, 1893), Vol. 2, pp. 340-2.
[3] §§ 22 and 24.

although they were necessary to make an error actual
heresy. This was especially true of the magisterium, which
was not so cut and dried as formal definition, and which
Newman had dealt with in section 17 of his pamphlet.[1]

In forwarding Errington's comments, Clifford added his
own. He interpreted Errington as objecting that while
Newman dealt with the ordinary and universal magisterium
of the Church in section 17, he did not sufficiently emphasize it when dealing with formal definitions in sections 4, 5
and 6. The fact that the Bishop did not expressly dissociate
himself from this criticism, while supporting Newman in
the case of some of the Archbishop's other objections, is
perhaps significant. Clifford, for example, did not agree with
Errington's objection to quoting the words of the Council
of Trent by which it was forbidden 'contra unanimem consensum Patrum ipsam Scripturam Sacram interpretari'.[2]
Nor did he agree with Errington that the phrase saying it
was never certain that there was not a double sense in
Scripture[3] was a 'very strong expression'.[4]

All the details of which Errington complained were modified. The passage on St Matthew, which Errington had
criticized for the same reasons as Clifford, was omitted. The
words 'acceptance of' the received opinion of St Paul's
authorship of the epistle to the Hebrews replaced 'acquiescence in'.[5] Newman spoke of man's writing being 'informed
and quickened' rather than 'spiritualized' by the presence
of the Holy Ghost.[6] He referred to Scripture having the
'nature' rather than the 'sacredness' of a Sacrament.[7]
Finally, when speaking of Scripture being inspired in all

[1] Errington to Clifford, 19 Oct 1883; VC 21.
[2] Originally quoted in § 17.
[3] Cf. § 20.
[4] Clifford to Newman, 22 Oct 1883; VC 21.
[5] § 25.
[6] § 22.
[7] § 18.

its parts which bear on faith, Newman concluded with the phrase 'including matters of fact', rather than with the theological expression he had originally used, *'res et sententias'*.[1]

None of these changes were of themselves very significant. Even the last one, which might at first sight seem an important one, did not change the sense of the section concerned, and the fact that Newman did not equate inspiration with inerrancy prevented this change from having the more extreme consequences which, taken in isolation and interpreted in an exaggerated form, it might have had. These changes are only important in so far as they can be seen as elucidations or clarifications restricting the freedom which Newman intended to show that the Catholic scholar enjoyed. Far more prejudicial to this attempt to treat the question of inspiration as an open one was the objection that opinions condemned under other theological terms could not be maintained without sinning against faith.

Newman first of all pointed out that he had never said 'maintained';

I have spoken of a Catholic investigator's *private* opinions (e.g. whether Adam lived 930 years which is not, I suppose 'dogma'). Hence I say 'the internal assent' §7 and §4, §5. A man may be doubtful what the Church has pronounced, whenever it is not actual dogma, and have haunting suspicions that perhaps he is opening his heart to unbelief, when the magisterium has not in fact settled a host of physical questions now any more than it had settled the question of the Solar System in the time of Galileo. I mean, while most priests could tell a man what

---

[1] § 13; Newman had previously used the phrase 'res et sententiae' and interpreted it as giving up the inspiration of every part, which obviously differs from his use of the phrase here. Cf. Seynaeve, p. 126*, note 2.

interpretations of Scripture were dogmatically forbidden,
few could pronounce what interpretations were forbidden
by the magisterium—and perhaps, as in the case of the
Fathers, few interpretations by the magisterium are
practically available for internal faith, unless singled out
and confirmed by dogma. In Scripture interpretation the
magisterium is infallible—is uninterrupted tradition
identical with the magisterium? if so, it is infallible too.
Is it?[1]

The point of Newman's argument was that the uninterrupted tradition of the Church could not be identified
with the ordinary and universal magisterium or teaching
of the Church because the former was not infallible.
Furthermore, unless the ordinary and universal magisterium of the Church was clear and certain, and in the case
under discussion it could only be so by formal definition,
there could be no obligation of faith. In other words, apart
from dogmatic definitions, all aspects of the subject of
inspiration must be treated as open questions. Newman
had no intention of allowing opinions to be 'maintained'
which had been condemned under other theological terms
or notes, but he was equally determined to avoid 'maintaining' stricter opinions in the question of inspiration than
was necessary. He was simply concerned with seeing and
showing to what extent the question was open, and patiently
waiting for the passage of time for the solution of remain-
ing problems.

By making it clear that he was simply contemplating the
inward peace of Catholics,[2] the Cardinal showed that he
did not allow condemned opinions to be 'maintained' without sinning against faith. He recognized the significance of

[1] Newman to Clifford, 25 Oct 1883; Clifton.
[2] § 7.

the magisterium by three changes: he removed the phrase
'or what is called dogma', from the final sentence of section
4; in section 5, he referred to section 17 and inserted the
phrase 'or the equivalent of dogma' into his conclusion;
finally, in section 18, Newman said that the Catholic scholar
must submit himself in matters of faith and morals 'to the
definite teaching', instead of 'to the judgement of Holy
Church'.

Another and more significant development which can be
traced is the final note on the phrase 'Auctor utriusque
Testamenti'. This note did not appear in the first printing
of the original pamphlet and did not form part of the
article in *The Nineteenth Century*. It can be found, in
W. P. Neville's handwriting, on the final pages of a copy of
the pamphlet,[1] and printed in what must be later copies of
the same pamphlet.[2] At this time, Newman considered that
his attempt to distinguish the 'Author of the Testaments or
Dispensations' from the 'Inspirer or Writer of the Books of
Scripture' was contrary to the definitions of the Vatican
Council, but when he published *Stray Essays*, he was no
longer convinced that this line of reasoning had been closed.

With the exception of this last development, all the other
changes can be traced and even dated. Newman marked
one copy of the pamphlet 'Sept 5 for the Press after corrections', in which he simply made the corrections necessary
for publication and did not make any of the changes under

---

[1] BOA, A.35.1, dated in Newman's hand 'Sept 1'.

[2] A.35.1, one copy dated 'Sept 5' and another 'Sept 6' in Newman's
hand. On another copy, Newman wrote 'State of the text as sent to the
Revisers for remark with note at the end'. He also added on p. 22
'Note at the end sent to Mr Adis [sic] April 1. 1884', A.13.2. Another
copy in the same bundle has the remark 'State of the text as sent to the
Revisers for remark with note as the end'. This copy was the one used
for comparison by the present Editors. A final copy catalogued under
A.28.7 bears Newman's comment 'As it went to the Revisers, but with
note at the end cut off'.

B*

discussion. These changes can be found in Neville's handwriting on an imperfect copy of the pamphlet dated 'after Sept. 5'. Finally Newman made the changes in his own hand on a copy on which the remark 'This is the authentic copy for publication Octr 26. 1883 JHN', is crossed out, and the distinct note 'JHN Sept 6. 1883', is retained. The October date coincides with the correspondence between Newman, Clifford and Errington, and the deleted remark probably originally meant exactly what it said.[1] The changes were also made in a copy of the pamphlet 'Read at the meeting of the Oxford Catholic Guild'[2] by Neville, for which Parkinson thanked Newman on November 22, 1883.[3]

In spite of the modifications which were made, the reaction to the pamphlet would probably have been much the same if it had been published in its original form as it was when published as the article in *The Nineteenth Century*. Clifford referred to the clear, careful and exhaustive manner in which Newman had treated the subject, which, he said, would be highly appreciated by all Catholics. This was especially true of the increasing number of Catholics involved in scientific research, who were often puzzled by the difficulties constantly brought forward from Scripture and the utter disregard or even contempt for scientific discoveries which was so frequently shown by those who defended religion and the inspired word of God.[4] Newman's appreciation of scientific criticism and its importance was a significant feature of the essay. A correspondent, who intended at an early opportunity to bring the article to the attention of the French public, wrote that his university friends in Paris were delighted with the article: 'it will give relief to hundreds—aye thousands of troubled minds'. He

[1] All three copies are catalogued under A.35.1.
[2] A.40.8.
[3] VC 21.
[4] Clifford to Newman, 7 Feb 1884; BOA, VC 21.

also sent a letter of appreciation from the French writer, Fouard.[1]

Very different was the reaction of Dr John Healy, a professor of theology at Maynooth, who was soon to be appointed Coadjutor Bishop of Clonfert, later succeeded to that see, and finally became Archbishop of Tuam. This hot-blooded defender of what he saw—somewhat narrowly —as orthodoxy rushed to arms and produced a reply, 'Cardinal Newman on the Inspiration of Scripture', in *The Irish Ecclesiastical Record* (of which he was editor) for March, 1884.[2] Though Newman's second article deals with the main points of Healy's argument, an ordered and less polemical summary is offered here.

Healy starts on a note of respectful courtesy, though even in the first paragraph there seems to be a barb in the phrase 'statements that are certainly calculated to startle even the veterans of the theological schools'—not the only passage which seems to voice a professional's resentment against one who is perhaps regarded, consciously or unconsciously, as an amateur who has received preferment above the professionals. In the next paragraph, as at the end, Healy somewhat condescendingly commends Newman's modesty in submitting all he writes to the judgement of the Church. After this the gloves are off. Healy begins by objecting to Newman's very phrasing of the objection which he set out to answer: then, concentrating on the Cardinal's treatment of inspiration, he offers what is intended as a brief summary of Newman's argument, giving the impression that his main point was the limitation of inspiration to matters of faith and morals, and concluding with the comment which particularly riled Newman, 'The merest tyro in the

[1] Hogan to Newman, 19 Feb 1884; Fouard to Hogan (probably), 13 Feb 1884; VC 21.

[2] Third Series, Vol. V (1884), pp. 137-49. Reprinted in Healy's *Papers and Addresses* (Dublin, 1909), pp. 404-17.

schools of Catholic theology will at once perceive the startling character of these statements, and the pregnant consequences which they involve.'

Healy admits that Newman acknowledges it to be *de fide*
that Scripture is inspired throughout, but charges him with
inconsistently asserting, at the same time, a restriction of
inspiration to matters of faith and morals. This, says Healy,
is based on an incorrect interpretation of the decrees of
Trent and Vatican I: he stresses the words of Trent requir-
ing 'libros ipsos integros cum omnibus suis partibus' to be
accepted 'pro sacris et canonicis', which phrase the Vatican
Council repeats and explains as meaning 'inspired'. Healy
concludes with a triumphant Q.E.D.

The professor's fire is next directed against Newman's
interpretation of the traditional phrase 'Deus auctor utriusque testamenti', as referring primarily to the two dispensations or covenants rather than the two collections of
books. Healy insists that in the decree of Trent, as in that
of Florence, the reference is to the books themselves, and
'auctor' has the sense of *literary* author. In all this no room
is allowed for any distinction such as that between 'matters
of fact' and 'matters of faith and morals'. Of course Newman is right in denying that God undertakes 'mere secular
duties' such as that of a 'historian or geographer': but the
point he has tried to make is better dealt with by the old
distinction between what is revealed *propter se* and what
is *per accidens*. Both, however, are revealed and imposed
on our faith: 'all serve a useful purpose in the divine
economy of our salvation'. Who can presume to decide what
things are worthy for God to reveal? Where is one to stop?

Healy now returns to Newman's positive, not restrictive,
assertion 'that faith and moral conduct is the "drift" of
the teaching that has the guarantee of inspiration'; he does
not object to this in itself, but insists that in the decree of

Trent it is subordinate to the 'main proposition' which implies 'the inspiration of every single statement made by sacred writers'. Indeed, the phrase 'tum ad fidem, tum ad mores pertinentes' refers to traditions, not to the books.

Passing now to inspiration and revelation, Healy charges Newman with not making the right distinction between them; inspiration necessarily implies revelation, but revelation is wider than inspiration. Newman, however, has confused them and made them 'contained in' Scripture, 'implying thereby, it seems to us, that all Sacred Scripture is not necessarily divine truth or a divine revelation, and that revelation and inspiration are identical'. Against such a view Healy disingenuously applies the words of Vatican I asserting that the sacred books are received by the Church not . . . 'merely because they contain revelation without error, but because they are inspired by the Holy Spirit and have God for author'. (Healy stresses 'contain', whereas the Council was rejecting a different view.) Healy concludes by proposing to give

a very brief explanation of the nature of inspiration as taught in all Catholic Schools, and as it is contained in the writings of the Fathers, and of all our eminent theologians, since the Council of Trent. Catholic teaching on this point has become still more definite and dogmatic since the definitions of the Council of the Vatican already referred to.

These words, breathing an evident desire to impose uniformity of thinking in the name of orthodoxy, introduce an account of the respective parts played by God and the human sacred writer which depends on the third thesis of Cardinal Franzelin's treatise De divinis Scripturis—an analysis which Franzelin, knowing that it was his own theory and not universal tradition, had rightly dissuaded the Fathers of Vatican I from adopting officially.

Healy finally shows he can make room for certain (purely literary) defects in Scripture, so as to distinguish his view from a 'divine dictation' theory, and he concludes by again congratulating the Cardinal on submitting his opinions to the authority of the Church.

Not to anticipate theological discussions which have their place below, it may be remarked here that Healy was correct in pointing out that neither Trent nor Vatican I defined, much less restricted, the 'drift' of what is taught by inspired Scripture: Newman had in fact taken the reference to 'matters of faith and morals' slightly out of context. But Healy did not ask himself sufficiently what was the question Newman was trying to answer: he does not seem to have seen the problem. He showed no historical sense at all, either in his criticism of Newman's explanation of 'auctor utriusque testamenti' or in his own acceptance of Franzelin's theory of inspiration as 'traditional'. Above all, the conflict was between a patient, deeply inquiring mind that wanted undecided questions left open and an impatient, intolerant spirit that regarded open questions as untidy, to be turned as soon as possible into static formulas that could be imposed as matters of faith.

Healy was not, however, the only person to criticize Newman, although he took the lead and probably influenced some who might otherwise have remained silent. The Bishop of Limerick claimed that a defence offered by Newman's friend Flanagan might be good as far as it went, but that it did not give the Cardinal a large enough loop-hole through which to escape, without crushing the life out of the essay. 'And what will it avail one like Newman to have escaped the mere note of heresy, if his answer to Renan is shown to be no answer, and his teaching as to the liberties

Biblical scholars may take with the inspiration of Scripture is shown to be misleading; and if his doctrine incurs all the other bad *notes* short of heresy.' The Bishop did not doubt that Newman would have a reply 'even at his fingers ends', but wondered whether he would publish it in *The Irish Ecclesiastical Record*. The attack on Newman's article bore the imprimatur of a brother Cardinal; would Newman's defence appear under the same imprimatur?[1]

The difficulties facing Newman can be seen in his correspondence with Clifford. He exemplified Healy's argument and understood him to maintain that although it was not *de fide* to believe that Nabuchodonosor was king of Nineveh, to refuse to believe it was inconsistent with accepting Scripture as the Word of God, the reason being that it was a certain proposition because an indisputable conclusion from a revealed premiss. Newman had no difficulty in answering Healy's point as a matter of reasoning or logic. He wanted to know, however, whether in fact it had been ruled that the statement, Nabuchodonosor was king of Nineveh, was an indisputable conclusion from *Scripture is the Word of God*. Was it necessarily inconsistent to believe that Scripture was wholly God's word, yet that he had not always spoken in that word in the case of secular facts? 'If the weight of authority in this particular case is so strong as to be decisive, I shall not appeal to logic.'[2]

Clifford replied that he himself did not think that it was inconsistent to regard Scripture as wholly the word of God while admitting that he had not always spoken in that word in the case of secular facts. He was forced to add, however, that the contrary opinion was stronger and the most common, and was shared, for example, by Errington. Clifford also pointed out that the Fathers and Schoolmen

[1] Bishop of Limerick to Flanagan, 5 Mar 1884; copy, VC 21.
[2] Newman to Clifford, 18 Mar 1884; Clifton.

strongly expressed the opinion that historical facts in Scripture must be accepted as true. His own solution was to distinguish between secular facts related 'per modum narrationis historicae' and those which were only referred to incidentally, and he questioned whether Scripture taught a fact or a supposed fact because it referred to it. In the case of Newman's example, the incident related in the Book of Judith 'per modum narrationis historicae' was that the king of Nineveh defeated the king of the Medes. The name Nabuchodonosor was incidentally mentioned and might simply have been a name used of him by the Jews at the time.[1] Newman's first difficulty, therefore, was that in replying to Healy he would have to oppose the common opinion in the Church.

The second difficulty was a practical one. Newman found that because of the rules of the magazine concerned and the laws of copyright, he could not reprint his original article in *The Nineteenth Century*, which he had intended to accompany his reply to Healy, until a year after publication.[2] He therefore had to issue a 'Postscript' to the article, with a 'Notice' explaining the circumstances.

When Newman reprinted his reply to Healy in *Stray Essays* he omitted, as he did in the case of Kingsley in later editions of the *Apologia*, all mention of Healy by name, referring instead to 'my Critic' or 'the Professor in question'. He also omitted a rather critical passage from his conclusion,[3] which had already been modified; the original draft read 'I am not daring to speak against any decision of the great doctors St Augustine and St Thomas, but I may be permitted to marvel at the lame reasoning offered in their support of one who, with so little preparation for such a

[1] Clifford to Newman, 24 Mar 1884; VC 22.
[2] Knowles (editor of *The Nineteenth Century*) to Newman, 1 Apr 1884; VC 22.
[3] Crossed out in proofs, BOA, A.40.8.

work, thinks it is his mission to deliver crude judgments upon a Cardinal of Holy Church.'[1]

Some correspondents, however, thought that Newman had not been hard enough. One of them wrote that Healy 'deserves all he has got—or will get, if the Postscriptum be published. Indeed I think His Eminence has let him off almost too easy.' The same writer wondered if it would be quite dignified for the Cardinal to reply to Healy and asked whether the task should not have been given to someone 'nearer the critic's own low level'.[2] Newman asked Clifford's opinion before publishing his reply and received a telegram of approval and a letter in which Clifford said that there could be no doubt of the 'thorough orthodoxy' of the Postscript which was 'a called for vindication' of Newman and his previous article. Clifford also considered that it was a very important and useful complement to the earlier article and that it would help still further in easing the minds and consciences of many good and thoughtful men.[3]

The reply received a great deal of support. Lord Emly told Newman of support for his views in France and for his reply to Healy from an Irish Jesuit.[4] One of the most interesting letters came from Friedrich von Hügel, who on other occasions showed himself critical of Newman's ideas and attitudes.[5] He wrote that the Rector of the Catholic Institute in Paris, Mgr d'Hulst, the Professor of Apologetics, de Broglie, and the Professor of Ecclesiastical History, Duchesne, had discussed Newman's papers and agreed with their conclusions. They all believed that Catholic apologetics would only be successful when the concessions

---

[1] A.45.1, in Neville's hand with Newman's corrections.
[2] O'Hanlon to Neville, 9 May 1884; VC 22.
[3] Clifford to Newman, 9 May 1884; also telegram, 9 May; VC 22.
[4] Lord Emly to Newman, 27 May 1884; VC 22.
[5] Cf. M. de la Bedoyère, *The Life of Baron von Hügel* (London, 1951), pp. 32-3.

which Newman allowed could be fully applied and explicitly proclaimed. For himself, von Hügel wrote:

> It is the repeated reading and study of your article with 'Postscript' on the Inspiration of Scripture which, following upon a five years study and consideration of the Greek New Testament text and modern commentaries of various German schools upon it, leads me to wish to thank you,—small as I know the value of such thanks to be,—for the profound interest and subtle help your papers have been to me personally.

A significant factor, once again, was Newman's acceptance of the results of criticism. Von Hügel was particularly grateful, for instance, for Newman's remarks that whether the last verses of St Mark and the two passages in St John were authentic did not affect their inspiration.[1]

Yet again, however, the reaction was not entirely favourable. One of the professors at St Bernard's Seminary near Birmingham liked the article in *The Nineteenth Century* and felt that Healy had been mistaken in taking up the subject at all, but he found Newman's reply 'over subtle'. He admitted that the Cardinal had done a service to the study of the extent of inspiration by bringing forward the theory of the *obiter dicta*, which while not new, had received less notice than it deserved. Furthermore, he also conceded that the theory was 'probable', in the theological sense of the word, namely that a Catholic was free to hold it. He explained, however, that he did not need the theory himself, nor did he personally have any leaning towards it or any sympathy with its spirit. He regarded it as 'a means of escape for the weaker brethren'. He also considered that people misunderstood Newman, who simply condescended to go as far as ever he could to aid the weak-

---

[1] Von Hügel to Newman, 1 Jul 1884; VC 22; cf. Essay I, § 24.

ness of others, whatever the largeness and exactness of his own faith. Understandably, he did not want Newman to read this letter.[1]

On the other hand, the general reaction was in Newman's favour. The Rector of Maynooth was sorry that Newman should have felt it necessary to appeal to his professors to take a charitable view of what he had done, and assured Newman of his deep regret that anything should have occurred to cause him so much pain.

> From the tone of the 'Postscript' it is plain to all that anything now written by Dr Healy to clear himself of the grave charges your Eminence has brought against him could not fail to make matters much worse than they are. I trust Dr Healy will take this view of the case, and prefer the merit of sacrifice involved in remaining silent, to any advantage he might hope to gain from any writing of his in defence of his article.[2]

Healy did in fact write and even print a second reply, surpassing the first both in length, in the warmth of his expressions of respect and regret for criticizing the Cardinal, and in the rigorism and dogmatism with which he tried to prove that Catholics had no freedom to hold a position such as he understood to be Newman's. He quoted copiously from theologians, mainly since the sixteenth century, and also from those passages of the Fathers which support the point he was hammering home. Healy agreed, however, not to publish the article, and he contented himself with printing in the *Irish Ecclesiastical Record* for June 1884 an 'Extract from Cardinal Franzelin on the Extent of the Inspiration of Scripture', to which he prefixed a short note explaining why he was not publishing his own article: 'It

[1] Parkinson to Pope, 22 May 1884; VC 22.
[2] Walsh to Newman, 27 May 1884; VC 22.

might perhaps aid doctrine, but it might also wound charity.'[1] Healy kept the article and published it twenty-five years later.[2] Few would judge that the cause of sound doctrine suffered by the delay, or was much advanced by the eventual publication.

One of the contributors to the issue of the *Irish Ecclesiastical Record* in which Healy's first attack had appeared considered it necessary to dissociate himself from the editor's article and wrote to express his regret. But he also excused his friend Healy, by reminding Newman that the magazine was Irish and ecclesiastical, and therefore pugnacious and hasty. He told Newman that while Healy was hot-headed, he was also warm-hearted and tended to be carried away by his own excitement and blinded by the dust he kicked up. Healy hammered away, perhaps enjoyed the strife, considering others as heedless as himself and feeling little the blows which he received. His better feelings prevailed when he cooled down and when he deeply regretted any expression which he might have used, but aware of his own good intentions, he found the greatest difficulty in understanding how he had given offence. Henry Bedford assured Newman that Healy regretted unintentionally offending him, and asked him to think more kindly of Healy than the latter's writings would lead him to do.[3]

Later in the same year, Healy was made a Bishop and Newman wrote through Walsh to offer him a present of a copy of the Canon of the Mass. Walsh replied that he had shown Newman's letter to several of the Irish Bishops, and told him that Healy was profoundly grateful and had some time previously decided to ask Newman's forgiveness for anything in the article which had offended or

---

[1] I.E.R., Third Series, V (1884), pp. 381-2.
[2] *Papers and Addresses* (Dublin, 1909), pp. 418-45.
[3] Bedford to Newman, 7 Jun 1884; VC 22.

annoyed him.[1] Newman then wrote directly to Healy:

My Dear Lord Bishop Elect,

I thank you for your kind message through Dr Walsh,
and for your acceptance from me of the offering which
I proposed to make to you.

That long life and a career of successful and happy
service in the Church of God may be granted to you
from above is the sincere prayer of

Your faithful servant
John H. Card. Newman.

P.S. This requires no immediate answer; you may be
going on retreat, and must have many occupations
besides.[2]

Healy thanked Newman and took the opportunity of expressing 'regret for any words which were calculated to
cause the least pain or annoyance' during their recent controversy and which he had certainly never intended. 'I
shall always regard that gift as a precious treasure, not
merely because it is a token of your Eminence's esteem for
me, but also because it is a striking proof of the nobility
and generosity of your own heart.'[3] Walsh was to have the
last word, however, when he wrote to tell Newman that
'In London last week when searching for something to give
as a suitable present to the new Bishop, I was fortunate
in finding a complete set of your Eminence's works, suit-
ably bound. There are 36 volumes in the set. I hope it is
complete.'[4]

[1] Walsh to Newman, 2 Jul 1884; VC 22.
[2] Newman to Healy, 3 Jul 1884; published in the closing footnote to
Healy's withheld second article, in his *Papers and Addresses*, p. 445.
Seynaeve, *Newman's Doctrine*, p. 79, prints the draft in the Birmingham
archives (VC 22).
[3] Healy to Newman, 17 Jul 1884; VC 22: published by Seynaeve,
Newman's Doctrine, p. 80.
[4] Walsh to Newman, 21 Aug 1884; VC 22.

III NEWMAN'S PLACE IN THE DEVELOPMENT OF THE CATHOLIC DOCTRINE OF INSPIRATION

1. *The Problems of Inspiration*

As soon as intelligent human beings believe that a personal God, their creator and the designer of their intellect, has communicated with them and that there exists a record of that communication, they are faced with a mystery full of problems. There is the problem of the possibility of revelation, of how the infinite God can communicate with man, since man can only understand with his finite mind and through human concepts and language. There is the problem of how a human book, evidently the product of a certain time and culture, and perhaps bearing the distinct imprint of a certain personality, can be held to be also the product of a divine communication. Since the image of God 'breathing on' the prophet or sacred writer has dominated the Judaeo-Christian tradition, this is called 'the problem of inspiration'. It involves the question of the relationship of the divine and human activities going to the production of a sacred book, and any explanation must cover, with sufficient psychological credibility, not only the exalted experience of the prophet in ecstasy but also the laborious editorial work of, say, the author of 2 Maccabees (recognized as inspired by Catholic tradition), who clearly did not feel inspired.

Further, there is the problem of the extent of inspiration. First, how many books are to be held products of biblical inspiration. The traditional answer is, as many books as first Judaism and then the Catholic Church recognized as 'canonical'. Since this recognition was only gradual and curiously haphazard, and was closely related to a parallel, gradually developing sense that certain books were 'inspired' and others were not, some care is needed to avoid making both the formulation of the question and the answer circular. Secondly, the problem of the extent of inspiration concerns not only the question 'which books' but also what we are to say about passages in books received as 'inspired' which seem trivial and unrelated to any conceivable divine inspiration.

Finally, there is the problem of 'inerrancy', which comes under the last-mentioned but is also of broader import. If the God who speaks is what Judaeo-Christian faith believes him to be, all-wise and all-good, then the books which we call his Word must be absolutely true: even though they are products of human minds, they must reflect the divine mind which cannot err or deceive, or else they fail as vehicles of his revelation. But Scripture contains many statements which appear to conflict with truths known from other sources; and the same problem is raised by conflicting accounts of the same event in different parts of Scripture. The difficulty is most acute for those who answer the problem of inspiration by a theory of divine 'dictation'. The knot may be cut by denying the inspiration of some passages, a course always rejected by orthodox tradition and Church councils: or explanation may be sought by developing a doctrine of different 'senses' of Scripture, so that when the obvious sense appears untrue or repugnant, a deeper, symbolic sense may be found which may satisfy a religious mind, and may be believed to express God's true intention. This expedient, much adopted by the Fathers, has always been recognized by Christian scholars

to be open to the danger of subjectivism: the first principle of interpretation is attention to what the sacred writer
can be ascertained to have intended. Consequently the
soundest approach to the problems of inerrancy is through
an investigation of the literary forms used by the authors
of biblical books. The fundamentalist refuses to discuss
different kinds of truth, but it is evident that different
literary forms do express truth in different ways. If (to
take an example which gave Newman unnecessary trouble)
the Book of Judith is a work of edifying fiction, the 'truth'
to be looked for in it is not that which we expect in the
Gospel Passion narratives.

These introductory remarks are offered to the reader
less deeply versed in the problems of inspiration, to help
him appreciate Newman's contribution, especially in the
two articles which are republished here. In fact Newman
contributed largely to the Christian understanding of many
of the problems referred to above, especially that of revelation, but we shall not attempt a general survey of his doctrine on Scripture, which would take us far beyond the
contents of the 1884 articles. The reader is referred to the
surveys by J. Seynaeve. Of the problems just mentioned,
those which chiefly concern us here are the relationship
of divine and human 'authors', the extent of inspiration
within the canonical books, and the scope of inerrancy,
with the various attempts at solving the latter problem.

2. The Divine and Human Authorship of Inspired Books

Newman, as we have seen, regarded the question of what
inspiration is as a very open one, at least till the First Vatican Council. The theology of inspiration has been developed
so much since Newman that we need to remind ourselves
how sketchy and unsatisfactory in fact were the current

notions up to his time (for the solution to be drawn from St Thomas still awaited development). Judaism, starting from the experience of prophecy, with the clear consciousness of receiving a message from God which it often entailed, traditionally maintained a 'dictation' theory, and many of the Church Fathers, expressing the role of the inspired writer through images such as that of a lyre on which God played, or the legend about St Gregory with the Holy Spirit in the form of a dove perched on his shoulder and cooing in his ear, failed to escape from this conception of the relationship of the human writer to God.[1] A 'dictation' theory may seem a natural account of some experiences of the prophets, but it is psychologically incredible when applied to St Luke writing his prologue or St Paul writing to Philemon.

The more scholarly among the Church Fathers, such as Origen and Chrysostom, were keenly aware of the real human authorship of a book of Scripture, but they did not leave the Church any clear theological explanation of its traditional faith in inspiration. St Thomas started from reflexions on prophetic inspiration in the light of his Aristotelian psychological theory and doctrine of causes, under the influence especially of the Arab philosophers and Moses Maimonides; St Thomas' explanation is in terms of joint causality, God being the principal cause and the human writer the instrumental cause. This theory was to be developed fruitfully in our day by M.-J. Lagrange and P. Benoit, by an analysis of what instrumental causality means when the 'instrument' is not a thing but a person, endowed with intellect and free will. But in the period after

---

[1] A convenient introduction to the Fathers' explanations of inspiration is R. M. Grant's *The Letter and the Spirit* (London, 1957). Newman summarized patristic theories in his 1861-3 notes; cf. Seynaeve, *Newman's Doctrine*, pp. 96*-105*.

St Thomas his hints were not followed up. A naïve dictation theory satisfied an age weak in biblical scholarship,
and when the Renaissance came to encourage such activity,
there was little but a bare assertion of the Church's traditional belief in inspiration to restrain scholars from treating Scripture just like any human book. The Council of
Trent in its *Decree on the Sacred Books* (in Session IV,
1546)[1] acted characteristically in making a declaration on a
point on which Protestants had departed from Catholic
tradition—the composition of the canon of Scripture—but
not on the nature of inspiration, which the Reformers had
not denied. Catholic scholars, who saw that the doctrine of
inspiration needed to be better explained in view of the
humanist attitude, but that a naïve dictation theory was
impossible, reacted so strongly against the latter as sometimes to give too small a place to the divine element. Thus
a discreet suggestion by L. Lessius (1586) that the assistance
of the Holy Spirit might perhaps in some case have been
given to move the Church to adopt as sacred a book written
in the ordinary human way, was carried farther by J. Bon-
frère (1625) and finally D. Haneberg (1850) went so far as to
say that the 'inspiration' of some books, e.g. the historical
books of the Old Testament, might mean no more than
this 'subsequent approval'. This view was explicitly censured
by the First Vatican Council, together with another insufficient theory, that of J. Jahn (1802) who had suggested that
inspiration meant simply 'negative assistance', a guarantee
of preservation from error. The Council's paragraph on
inspiration in the Dogmatic Constitution *Dei Filius, de fide
catholica*, chapter 2, *De Revelatione*, contained the first
attempt at an explanation of inspiration. Revelation, the
passage says, is contained, as Trent had said,[2] 'in the written

[1] Denz. 783-6 [1501-8 in Schönmetzer's new edition].
[2] Denz. 783 [1501].

books and unwritten *traditiones*'[1] handed down by the Apostles, and the full canon of Scripture is as defined at Trent (itself merely repeating one of the documents of Florence).[2] The Vatican text then continues:

Eos vero Ecclesia pro sacris et canonicis habet, non ideo, quod sola humana industria concinnati, sua deinde auctoritate sint approbati; nec ideo dumtaxat, quod revelationem sine errore contineant; sed propterea, quod Spiritu Sancto inspirante conscripti Deum habent auctorem, atque ut tales ipsi Ecclesiae traditi sunt.	But the Church holds them sacred and canonical not only as being approved by her authority after having been written by purely human efforts (Haneberg) nor on the sole grounds of their containing revelation without error (Jahn); but because being written under the inspiration of the Holy Spirit, they have God as their author, and as such they have been given to the Church.[3]

The explanation, such as it is, is in the last sentence. It uses the traditional term *auctor* in an apparently tradi-

[1] The word is left in Latin in order not to prejudge how it is to be understood in the Vatican text. At Trent, as M. Bévenot has shown ('Traditiones in the Council of Trent' in *The Heythrop Journal*, IV [1963], pp. 333-47), the word should be rendered 'observances', and does not refer to tradition as a source of revelation. The Vatican Fathers were, however, probably unaware of this. This point about Trent should be borne in mind in considering Newman's argument about faith and morals as the 'drift' of inspiration, for in the text of Trent the phrase about faith and morals occurs as a qualification of *traditiones*, 'observances', and cannot therefore be given the theological significance which Newman wished.

[2] The *Decree for the Jacobites* (1442), Denz. 706 [1334-5].

[3] Denz. 1787 [3006], the writer's translation. The passage is referred to by Newman in Essay I, § 24, n. 2. One of Healy's most unjust arguments involved giving the passage an emphasis not intended by the Council in order to discredit Newman.

tional way: the phrase 'Deus auctor utriusque Testamenti' had a long history before it appeared in the Tridentine decree, from which the Vatican decree was apparently quoting it. But in fact a certain change of emphasis had taken place, due to the work of J. B. Franzelin (1816-1886), an Austrian Jesuit who lectured in theology in the Roman College from 1857 to 1876, when he was made a cardinal. In his treatise *De divina Traditione et Scriptura*[1] he had developed the idea of God's authorship of Scripture in such a way as, he thought, to strike a mean between an exaggerated dictation theory and a minimizing theory of 'negative assistance'. Franzelin's theory was, put crudely, that God inspired the human author with the matter to be revealed, but that the human author was responsible for the form of expression, and in this was free to be himself, subject only to 'negative assistance' or preservation from error. Thus it could truly be said that a man was author (a proposition which no one would wish to deny) and yet God was author too, and tradition provided a useful tag to support this. Franzelin's theory had a great success. He was responsible for drafting the schema on revelation at the First Vatican Council, and was called in to expound it; the paragraph reproduced above represents two theses of his treatise, the fourth (insufficiency of the theories of subsequent approval and negative inspiration) and the second, 'The books of Scripture are inspired in such a way that God is their author'. Franzelin, however, with a true theologian's humility and sense of responsibility, dissuaded the Fathers from giving authoritative force to his personal theory about the respective roles of God and the human author. This was fortunate, for it was soon to come under an attack which it could not survive; Lagrange and his school criticized its impossible 'psychological vivisection'

---

[1] Ed.1, Rome, 1870 (just after the Council); ed.2 (revised), Rome, 1875.

and pointed out that in effect it merely put divine dictation side by side with human activity under divine assistance, failing to give a unified account of authorship. In
place of this Lagrange proposed, and Benoit developed, a
revival of the Thomist theory.[1] But this takes us too far
beyond Newman.

Newman, as we have seen, and as the 1884 articles illustrate, combined the traditional Christian belief that the
Bible is the word of God with the scholar's feel for the
biblical books as human documents. No theory of inspiration which undermined the reality of human authorship
could have satisfied him. Thus in the 1861-3 papers we find
him considering the dictation theory to reject it;[2] he
thought that if God's 'authorship' is said to mean *literary*
authorship, this entails an undesirable division: 'then there
will be two writers of the Scriptures, the divine and the
human'.[3] Rather than regard inspiration as primarily a
quality of *books* (as fundamentalists will always do), Newman preferred to say (and understood Trent to say):

> The Divine Inspirer, inasmuch as He acted on the
> writer, acted, not immediately on the books themselves,
> but through the men who wrote them. The books are
> inspired, because the writers were inspired to write them.
> They are not inspired books, unless they came from
> inspired men.[4]

This way of describing the relationship of God and the

---

[1] Cf. P. Synave and P. Benoit, *Prophecy and Inspiration* (1947, Eng.
tr. New York 1961) P. Benoit, *Inspiration and the Bible* (1963, Eng. tr.
London 1965).

[2] Seynaeve, *Newman's Doctrine*, p. 126*. Newman reviews theories,
including those of 'dictation', 'approbation' and 'assistance', ibid.,
pp. 108*-12*.

[3] Essay I, § 10. The comment anticipates criticism of Franzelin's
theory, which, however, Newman probably did not know.

[4] Essay I, § 19.

human author clearly safeguards better the latter's real authorship:

> Being inspired because written by inspired men, they have a human side, which manifests itself in language, style, tones of thought, character, intellectual peculiarities, and such infirmities, not sinful, as belong to our nature.[1]

The product of this co-operation by 'A divine *Auctor* and a human *Scriptor*' is a book which Newman liked best to think of as a sort of sacrament, a special case of the sacramental principle which he saw in operation throughout God's creation. This view of Scripture is found in the papers of 1861-3[2] and is briefly referred to in the 1884 articles.[3] Already St Augustine[4] and the *Imitation of Christ*[5] had compared Holy Scripture to the Eucharist, and the same comparison is adopted (as we shall see at the end of this essay) by Vatican II, in the Constitutions on the Liturgy and on Revelation.

It was thus in a broad and 'sacramental' sense that Newman understood Scripture to have God for its author. He did not believe that the traditional phrase 'Deus auctor utriusque Testamenti' must be interpreted as 'God is the "literary" author of both the old and the new collections of biblical books'; in fact he did not regard the phrase as enshrining a doctrine of inspiration, but only as having been adapted to refer to inspiration by the Vatican Council. It is curious that Newman and Franzelin were studying

[1] Essay II, § 30.
[2] Seynaeve, *Newman's Doctrine*, pp. 127*-8*, with Seynaeve's comment, pp. 132-3.
[3] Essay I, § 18.
[4] Augustine interprets 'our daily bread' in terms of both Eucharist and Word of God in this 'sacramental' sense in his sermons, 56, 10; 58, 4; 59, 3 (PL 38, 389; 395; 401).
[5] *Imitation* IV, 11, 4.

the phrase at about the same time; but as Newman never mentions Franzelin's teaching in any work that remains to us, it is doubtful whether he knew it. Franzelin's discussion, in his second thesis on Scripture,[1] includes a list of Church documents, going back from Trent and Florence, but shows a certain lack of historical sense and no awareness that the phrase had started life expressing a different point from his own, as a statement against dualist heretics who rejected the God of the old covenant and therefore also the Old Testament. Basing himself more on later documents, where the phrase introduces the list of canonical books, Franzelin argued for the stricter sense of 'literary author' which he wanted, rather than its original broader connotation, and took 'testamentum' in the sense of a collection of books rather than the original sense of 'covenant' or 'dispensation'. On this basis he was able to commend his own theory of divine and human authorship as more traditional than it was.

Meanwhile Newman also was studying the phrase 'Deus auctor utriusque Testamenti' to see what light it could throw on the problem of inspiration. In 1861 he copied out and carefully studied all the Church documents he could find bearing on inspiration, including most of those that contain this phrase.[2] He reproduced the latter data in the 'Note' following the first 1884 article, where also he summarized his conclusions.[3] Newman saw that the sense of the phrase was originally anti-dualist rather than expressing the doctrine of inspiration: the stress was originally on 'utriusque' (of both) rather than on 'auctor'. The idea, if not the words, came from Irenaeus, who argued forcibly in this way against the Marcionites: 'testamentum' was to

[1] *De divina Traditione et Scriptura*, ed. 1, pp. 284-6; ed. 2, pp. 334-6.
[2] Seynaeve, *Newman's Doctrine*, pp. 76*-84*.
[3] § 29 (Note); §§ 9, 10 etc.

be taken not only in the sense of a part of the Bible but more broadly, as the whole ancient dispensation which they rejected. 'The phrase then . . . does not mean that "God inspired the whole Bible", but that "the Mosaic Covenant as well as the Christian has come from the One God"'.[1] The phrase was adopted, apparently in Spain, to counter the Priscillianists, and became regular in professions of faith, both those taken by bishops at their consecration[2] and those imposed on heretics or schismatics returning to union. While, as Newman failed to observe, a sense of 'Deus auctor' implying 'inspirer' does appear in the Fathers from the time of Ambrose and Augustine, the Tridentine decree is the first Church document which suggests any interest in this sense of the phrase: and Vatican I is the first to make it primary. After Vatican I Newman hesitated whether it was still permissible to take the classical phrase in a broad sense. Healy attacked Newman's interpretation, basing himself on Franzelin (including Franzelin's third thesis, to which he could not legitimately appeal as defined by Vatican I).

This helped Newman to make up his mind. He published the 'Note' in Stray Essays, but in place of the modest

[1] Seynaeve, Newman's Doctrine, p. 81* (BOA A.11.11, p. 153). The disjunction is too hard. The exhaustive study of the patristic use of the phrase by A. Bea (the future Cardinal), 'Deus auctor Sacrae Scripturae: Herkunft und Bedeutung der Formel', in Angelicum XX (1943), pp. 16-31, shows that at least the fourth century anti-Manichaean writers, such as Augustine and Serapion of Thmuis, did intend to include, in expressions of this kind, the sense of God inspiring the whole Bible, and that this sense was frequent from St Gregory on. Bea concludes that the adaptation of the phrase by Vatican I, omitting any stress on 'both testaments' is 'a shift of emphasis which is without significance for the concept of author'. One may agree that the shift had been prepared for longer than Newman realized, but his point remains valid, that 'auctor' had originally had a broader sense, and that we are not obliged to restrict it to the 'literary' sense.

[2] This use appears first in the Statuta Ecclesiae Antiqua, Denz. (Schönmetzer's edition only) 325, a south Gaulish document of the mid- or late fifth century, not in Newman's list.

disclaimer, 'The above is only noted historically, for the Vatican Council has defined Auctor Testamenti to be Auctor Scripturarum', Newman now decided he could admit this definition and interpret it in his sense of inspiration, concentrating on faith and morals.

Was such an interpretation of the Vatican text permissible? Abbot Butler, in a discussion of the phrase 'auctor utriusque Testamenti' (in which surprisingly he never refers to Newman),[1] considers that the magisterium has not committed itself to the divine 'authorship' (in a quasi-literary sense) of the Scriptures quite as finally as to their inspiration, but 'with everything short of that absolute finality'. But, continues the Abbot,

> in view of the history of the concept of divine authorship in magisterial pronouncements, it could be argued that the Vatican Council's use of the word 'author' in this connection is to be interpreted with more emphasis on the idea of the supernatural provenance of the books than on the precise idea of 'literary' authorship.

The Encyclical *Providentissimus Deus*, however, is quite explicit, 'but it could be pointed out that an Encyclical has not exactly the same authority as an ecumenical definition'.[2]

Newman, in continuing to maintain, in accord with his historical sense and understanding of the development of doctrine, a broad interpretation of God's 'authorship' of Scripture, stands out today as a lone voice in favour of a psychologically credible view of inspiration, in an age when the whole chorus was singing with Franzelin, whose theory the Encyclical *Providentissimus Deus* of 1893 was to propound absolutely, as Vatican I had not done.

[1] D. J. B. Hawkins and the Abbot of Downside, 'A Suggestion about Inspiration', in *The Downside Review* LXXX (1962), pp. 197-213 the Abbot's discussion of the phrase in question is on pp. 204-9.

[2] Art. cit., pp. 208-9.

C

Vatican II, in the Constitution *De Divina Revelatione*, has repeated the words of Vatican I, but has ventured farther, with the first conciliar text ever to propose any account of how inspiration 'worked'. The sentence reflects the modern development of the Thomist theory of instrumental causality, as it had already been commended in the Encyclical *Divino Afflante Spiritu* (1943): it shows a concern not to prejudice free theological discussion of open questions which would have delighted the heart of Newman (but not of Healy!) and which is repeatedly reflected in the 'relationes' (reports by the drafting committees) of Vatican II. The sentence itself would surely have received Newman's warm approval:

In sacris vero libris conficiendis Deus homines elegit, quos facultatibus ac viribus suis utentes adhibuit, ut Ipso in illis et per illos agente, ea omnia eaque sola, quae Ipse vellet, ut veri auctores scripto traderent.	In producing the sacred books God chose men and employed them, using their own faculties and powers, in such a way that He acted in and through them, and they committed to writing all that, and only what, He willed, while being themselves authors in the true sense.[1]

The following sentence comes even more evidently close to Newman's thought, but it will be considered below.

In conclusion of this section, it cannot be said that Newman offered a coherent account of how inspiration 'worked', but his hints have proved, perhaps, more fruitful for the development of the doctrine of inspiration than Franzelin's theory. On the present question, Newman's most important contribution is his insistence on keeping questions open

[1] Chapter III, section 11 (the writer's translation).

despite the efforts of theologians of a certain over-dogmatic temper, and his historical study of 'Deus auctor'. Negative as the result of this study may appear at first sight, it reveals an instance of what can happen in the development of doctrine: a consecrated phrase may receive a new emphasis, and an answer to a new question may be put forward as traditional.[1]

Newman knew how far the doctrine of inspiration had developed in his day and how far it had not. The broader sense of 'Deus auctor' for which he held out makes him in a way the ancestor—albeit unacknowledged—of those modern theories which have tried to stand back from the detailed analysis of the process of inspiration, and to put it in a broader context. Thus Karl Rahner in his brilliant essay *Inspiration in the Bible*,[2] though, when he discusses the definition of God's 'authorship' (without reference to Newman) he makes no difficulty about accepting the 'literary author' sense analogously,[3] effectively broadens the sense so as to make God's 'authorship' of Scripture merely one aspect of his 'authorship' of the Church, thus leaving room for real human authorship under his guidance. Again, those scholars who, following Rahner, have considered inspiration as a charism guiding a long, developing, largely anonymous tradition in God's people as well as composition by individual authors,[4] may be seen as following

[1] Cf. Essay I, § 6. Reflecting on these lines, it may be asked whether the present theological *impasse* about the use of marriage is not due to an error of this kind: the questions being asked in the light of a newly flowering doctrine of the human person and of interpersonal relations can hardly be settled summarily by appeal to documents which were written envisaging other contexts and problems.

[2] Original German 1958; Eng. tr., ed. 2, in *Studies in Modern Theology* (London, 1966), which should be used in preference to the first translation, published in 1961.

[3] *Studies in Modern Theology*, pp. 13-14.

[4] E.g. J. L. McKenzie, 'The Social Character of Inspiration', in *Myths and Realities* (London, 1963), pp. 56-69; D. J. McCarthy, 'Personality, Society and Inspiration', in *Theological Studies* 24 (1963), pp. 553-76.

a line which Newman's flexible position was capable of opening up. This is, however, a *post eventum* judgment: Newman's theory did not in fact have the influence it might have had, both because of the success of Franzelin's and because of the misunderstanding that has dogged Newman's theory almost ever since. To this we now turn.

3. *The Extent of Inspiration*

While, as Newman saw when in 1861 he was studying the documents of the Church, nothing had been explicitly defined about inspiration up to that time, inspiration was implicitly understood to be coextensive with the canon of Scripture as received by the Catholic Church. Trent declared that 'the entire books with all their parts' are to be held 'sacred and canonical';[1] Vatican I, repeating this, explicitly gave the reason—because they are inspired.[2] Healy judged it necessary to instruct Newman on this point, since Newman appeared to be restricting the extent of inspiration. But Newman was well aware of the force of Tradition, as his 1861-3 notes show. In his answer to Healy he acknowledged 'These two Councils decide that the Scriptures are inspired, and inspired throughout'.[3] Newman understood Healy's thesis perfectly well, but regarded it as concerned with a different point from that which interested him. 'If this is his position, it is plain that I approach the question on quite a distinct side from his; but I do not see that personally and practically I have very much to differ from him in. . . .'[4] Since Healy had made his point adequately, the tedious and interminable piling up of authorities in his (withheld) second article was a waste of time.

[1] Canon, Denz. 784 [1504].
[2] Denz. 1787 [3006]; Canon, Denz. 1809 [3029].
[3] Essay II, § 30, and even more explicitly in § 36.
[4] Cf. Essay II, § 31.

Newman simply was not much interested in what we may call the 'material' extent of inspiration, as coextensive with canonicity. He venerated the whole of Scripture as sacred and the Word of God. His delicacy of feeling made him apologize for 'seeming to use light words on a sacred subject' in his playful irony about St Paul's cloak.[1] But he realized that if we are to stop at that sense of inspiration which applies to every verse of the Bible, we shall be in danger of making inspiration mean very little; the Word of God to man cannot be concerned with the whereabouts of cloaks. God inspired human authors in order to make them the agents and their works the vehicles of his revelation, for the salvation of mankind, not to teach men history or geography.[2] A note written in 1861 shows Newman aware of the distinction between inspiration as an attribute of all Scripture, and as the charism operating for God's special purposes:

> I am supposing as true the theory of a plenary inspiration extending throughout the whole volume and every part of it, but operating only there for religious objects, just as a lamp might illuminate a surface, without imparting to it warmth.[3]

In the second 1884 article Newman expressly accepted the coextensiveness of inspiration with the canon, as defined by Vatican I,[4] yet he persisted in speaking of inspiration as restricted to 'the special object with reference to which the sacred writers were endowed with the gift'. Why, if he accepted the distinction between these senses of

[1] Essay II, § 34, 2.
[2] Cf. Essay I, § 11.
[3] Seynaeve, *Newman's Doctrine*, p. 137* (BOA A.35.5, p. 5 of MS A, at left-hand side). It must be stressed that this is a very rough note and Newman regards the position as a 'hypothesis'. It is referred to here in order to substantiate that Newman was aware of the distinction.
[4] Essay II, § 36.

inspiration, did he not use clearer terminology? It would have saved him, and theologians since his death, not a little trouble. The answer is, that Newman believed that inspiration had been defined by the Church in terms of its relationship to revelation, and in particular to 'matters of faith and morals', rather than in terms of its 'material' extent. This is why he was satisfied with very general expressions of reverence for Scripture as being throughout the Word of God, but he concentrated on what he understood inspiration to be *about* and *for*.

Newman argued, therefore, that Trent and Vatican I 'specify "faith and moral conduct" as the drift of that teaching which has the guarantee of inspiration';[1] further, 'Scripture is inspired, not only in faith and morals, but in all its parts which bear on faith, including matters of fact'.[2] We find him interpreting the decree of Trent in this sense already in the 1861-3 notes.[3] Was he justified?

Newman says that Trent insists four times on 'faith and morality' as the scope of inspired teaching.[4] The first two instances occur in the long paragraph on revelation[5] (though the word is not used), as contained in the Church's Gospel, handed down from Christ and the Apostles, 'tamquam fontem omnis et salutaris veritatis et morum disciplinae' (Newman renders this 'the fount of all saving truth and all instruction in morals'). This 'truth and instruction' is contained in Scripture and in the unwritten 'traditiones' (which in the Tridentine context should be understood as 'observances')[6] taught by Christ or by the

---

[1] Essay I, § 11. For the exact meaning of the terms, cf. M. Bévenot, ' "Faith and Morals" in the Councils of Trent and Vatican I' in *The Heythrop Journal* III (1962), pp. 15-30.

[2] Essay I, § 13.

[3] Seynaeve, *Newman's Doctrine*, p. 83*.

[4] Essay I, § 12.

[5] Denz. 783 [1501].

[6] See the study by M. Bévenot referred to on p. 53, n. 1.

Holy Spirit and handed down by the Apostles: therefore the Council accepts with equal love and reverence 'all the books of both the Old and the New Testaments, since one and the same God is "author" of both, and also the observances, whether relating to faith or to moral conduct' (nec non traditiones ipsas, tum ad fidem, tum ad mores pertinentes), as taught either orally by Christ or by the guidance of the Holy Spirit, and handed down in the Church.

Though Trent here envisages the entire vehicle of revelation which is entrusted to the Church as, broadly speaking, the product of inspiration, it cannot be said that either reference to 'faith and morals' is directly related to scriptural inspiration as such. Indeed, the second time the phrase is used it qualifies 'traditiones' and that not restrictively but rather in order to widen the reference of the term.

Newman's third instance is from the end of this section on the Sacred Books, in which the Council calls attention to the principles by which it is proceeding 'for the confirmation of dogmas and the establishment of morals in the Church'.[1] Here 'matters of faith and morals' are mentioned to sum up the scope of the Church's teaching mission; nothing is said about scriptural inspiration.

The last instance cited by Newman, and later reproduced by him together with the virtual repetition of it by Vatican I, is in the following section of Trent on the 'authenticity' of the Vulgate and the duty of interpreting Scripture with the Church, not by private judgment alone.[2] Here the Councils specify the field in which it is most important that Catholics should conform to the 'mind of the Church' in interpreting Scripture; 'faith and morals' are the special

---

[1] Denz. 784 [1505].
[2] Essay I, § 16. Trent, Denz. 786 [1507]; Vatican, 1788 [3007].

province of the teaching Church. Thus here the context is about the limitations of freedom in interpreting Scripture, not about the scope of inspiration of Scripture.

We must conclude, then, that Newman did not interpret Trent rightly in taking its references to 'faith and morals' as expressing in any way a restriction of the scope of inspiration: on this, it must be recognized, Healy criticized Newman correctly. He accepted Newman's specification of 'matters of faith and morals' as the 'drift' or 'scope' of inspired teaching, but showed that the decree of Trent does not allow any *restriction* of inspiration to such matters; rather, it implicitly affirms that every book and every part is inspired.[1]

There is no doubt that the passages to which Newman appealed do mean that revelation, as it is transmitted to us by the Church, is about what we must believe and how we must live. But they say it quite broadly, not by way of definition, much less of restriction. The references to Christ and the Holy Spirit can also be said to express the notion of inspiration in a broad sense. Therefore it is acceptable (and was so even to Healy) to make a broad positive statement such as that inspiration is concerned primarily with matters of doctrine to be believed and of Christian conduct. It is acceptable, again, to say that inspiration was given to teach men not history or geography but truth necessary for salvation. Thus St Thomas, speaking really of inspiration though in terms of prophecy, applies the Aristotelian principle of finality and says that here too the matter is determined by the purpose:

Hence all those things the knowledge of which is useful to salvation are matter of prophecy, whether they are

[1] J. Healy, 'Cardinal Newman and Inspiration', in *Papers and Addresses* (Dublin, 1909), pp. 411-12.

past, future or eternal, necessary or contingent. But those things which cannot concern salvation do not belong to the matter of prophecy: hence Augustine says . . . 'Though our authors knew what shape the sky is, the Spirit did not wish to declare through them any truth except what is profitable for salvation'. . . . By 'necessary for salvation' I mean necessary either for the instruction of faith or for moral training.[1]

This passage would have served Newman very well if he had quoted it in his 1884 essays. But it would have been necessary for him to make clearer than he did that such statements are about the purpose for which God gave the charism of inspiration; one should not speak about the sacred text itself in such a way as to suggest that some parts are inspired and some are not. With Catholic Tradition we must say that *all* is to be called inspired, but we may say that not every part of Scripture need be considered an actual means of revelation.[2] Newman ran into difficulties because he used 'inspired' rather in this latter sense (of an actual means of revelation) without distinguishing it expressly from 'inspired', meaning simply part of the sacred text: he limited the scope of inspiration in the sense in

[1] *De Veritate* q. 12, art. 2, corpus. The passage from St Augustine, which St Thomas quotes only loosely, is in *De Genesi ad Litteram* II, 9 (PL 34, 270-1). Cf. ibid. II, 10. These passages are quoted by Vatican II in treating of inspiration and inerrancy, as we shall see.

[2] Healy criticized Newman for not introducing the distinction between inspiration and revelation (art. cit., pp. 412-13) but proposed it himself in a curiously unhelpful way. The implicit distinctions in Newman's thought were analysed much more satisfactorily by V. McNabb in his sympathetic and penetrating article 'Cardinal Newman and the Inspiration of Scripture' in *Where Believers may Doubt* (London, 1903), pp. 31-50, reprinted again in *Frontiers of Faith and Reason* (London, 1937), pp. 65-77. Seynaeve, however, criticizes McNabb's analysis (*Newman's Doctrine*, pp. 178-9) and concludes, rightly, that Newman's position was rather confused.

C*

which he was interested in it, and ventured not only to define its scope but also to specify the sort of matter in Scripture which does not seem an actual means of revelation. It was for such passages that he used the celebrated expression 'obiter dicta'—things said 'in passing' and not with the deliberation given to the main point one is making.[1] Newman, whether or not with justice to his overall position, has gone down into doctrinal history as holding that there are 'obiter dicta' in Scripture and that they are not inspired because not related to faith or morals.

This was the opinion—expressing St Thomas' teaching in somewhat bold and slightly untraditional language, but never condemned—of William Holden, an English theologian who taught at the Sorbonne in the seventeenth century, in his *Analysis of Divine Faith*. The contemporary translation reads:

> Fourthly, that the special and Divine assistance which is given to the author of every such book as the Church receives for the Word of God, doth only extend itself to those things which are doctrinal, or at least have some neer or necessary relation unto them. But in those things which are written by the bye, or have reference to something else not concerning Religion, I conceive, the author had only such a Divine assistance as other holy and saintly authors have.[2]

Newman seems to have read Holden in Rome in 1846, when he wrote: 'It is worth reading, though it has acknowledged faults—and I like Perrone better'.[3] The references to Holden in the 1861-3 papers are only through

---

[1] See Essay I, § 26 for Newman's explanation of the term.

[2] *The Analysis of Divine Faith* (Paris, 1658), p. 61; original Latin, *Divinae Fidei Analysis* (Paris, 1652), p. 82.

[3] Newman to Penny, 13 Dec 1846; *Letters and Diaries* XI, p. 293.

mentions by Perrone, as representing a 'negative assistance' theory of inspiration. Yet Newman possessed a copy of Holden, bought probably between 1846 and 1850, and still at Birmingham. It is curious that he never acknowledges the similarity of his 'obiter dicta' to Holden's expression.

Newman's purpose in drawing attention to 'obiter dicta' seems to have been twofold: to emphasize the central revealed message of Scripture—that for which it was inspired —as against the details which often stick in people's imagination and memory, but are not of that central importance; and secondly, to provide a means of solving the problems raised for believers by passages which in their apparent surface meaning are not true. Newman proposed to satisfy this twofold purpose by saying that 'obiter dicta' are not inspired, in his special sense of 'inspired'. But he risked running foul of the general Catholic understanding of two principles: that Scripture is inspired throughout, and that it is inerrant throughout. He could have satisfied his first purpose, and finally did, by saying clearly that Scripture is inspired throughout, but that inspiration is only fully engaged in the work for which it was given, when part of God's revelation is being expressed.[1] In pursuit of his second purpose, to solve problems of the 'truth' of Scripture, Newman did well to draw attention to certain statements, such as that about Nabuchodonosor in the book of Judith, and point out that they are without much importance for revelation; but the problem is better solved, as the Church has now recognized, by another method.

[1] This is better expressed in a passage in the 1861-3 notes (Seynaeve, *Newman's Doctrine*, p. 140*) than ever in the 1884 articles: Newman says St Paul was an inspired man all the time, but 'there is more place for inspiration to act' in the passages containing revealed doctrine, than when e.g. he writes about his friends or about his cloak and books (BOA A.35.5, p. 147 of MS B).

4. *The Inerrancy of Scripture*

Newman was much annoyed with Healy for interpreting his theory of 'obiter dicta' as implying that these less significant passages in Scripture were not subject to the charism of inerrancy and might therefore contain error.

> Why does he always associate an *obiter dictum* with the notion of error or moral infirmity, or even, as he sometimes expresses himself, with *'falsehood'*? At least what right has he to attribute such an association to me? I have implied no such thing.[1]

Healy, however, cannot be called entirely unfair for using this weapon. In Christian Tradition the belief that the Bible is inspired by God has always entailed, at least implicitly, the belief that therefore God's infallible veracity is reflected in the text of the Bible. Inspiration entails inerrancy. Restrict inspiration within the sacred books, and you restrict inerrancy, allowing the possibility of some part of the Bible containing 'error'. So Healy argued, and his argument was as traditional and familiar as his insistence that every word of Scripture is inspired. He saw Newman's theory of 'obiter dicta', however well meant, as leading to the pitfalls for faith about which St Augustine had lectured St Jerome, on account of the latter's dangerous suggestion that perhaps St Paul had only pretended to reprove St Peter:

> It is one question whether a good man may ever tell an untruth, but quite another whether a writer of Holy Scripture could be allowed to tell one. Or rather it is not 'another question'; the question simply does not arise.

[1] Essay II, § 34, 2.

For if even a 'white lie' is once admitted in this very summit of authority, no part of those books will remain which cannot be ascribed, on the same pernicious principle, to the author's untruthful intention and purpose, whenever anyone finds something either difficult to obey or impossible to believe.[1]

Or, as St Augustine warns even more dramatically elsewhere: 'Faith will totter, if the authority of the divine Scriptures wavers: and when faith totters, charity itself wilts.'[2] Healy saw Newman's theory as threatening to raise this spectre, and he reacted like a good Irishman. Newman was irritated, but he could not complain with full justification. Whether he intended it or not, he *had* raised the question of inerrancy, and his case had to be tried at this bar. Healy's insistence on the 'material' coextensiveness of inspiration with every book and every part of the Bible was well based in tradition and Church documents, and so was his understanding of the corresponding doctrine of inerrancy—even if it had not yet been explicitly defined.[3] Of course what was needed was further analysis of inerrancy, to distinguish in what sense 'the Bible is true'. Newman accepted the doctrine of inerrancy as faithfully as he accepted plenary inspiration; but just as he was asking a different question about inspiration, the question he was raising about inerrancy was not that of its total extent, but that of its meaning. This question arises as soon as one takes

---

[1] Letter 28, 3; PL 33, 112-13; CSEL 34, p. 108.
[2] *De Doctrina Christiana* I, 37; PL 34, 35.
[3] Vatican I, in declaring inadequate the view of inspiration which reduced it to a guarantee of inerrancy (Denz. 1787 [3006]), is the first council to mention inerrancy explicitly, but even here it is (in another sense of the phrase) an 'obiter dictum', being expressed in the subjunctive. Vatican II is the first council to publish a clear statement of the traditional doctrine: the text will be considered below.

seriously the Christian belief that the Bible is God's word, yet spoken through human agents. God's word must be true: but the human statements quite often seem untrue, at least in their immediate surface meaning. A fundamentalist will refuse to discuss the question, or will give superficial answers which often raise more difficulties than they solve. A thinking Christian must try to penetrate deeper into the question, in what does the 'truth' of Scripture consist?

The problem arises in two principal ways: from the discrepancies of Scripture passages with each other, and from the discrepancies of scriptural statements with our knowledge from other sources. An example of the first difficulty is found in the gospel accounts of Jesus' healing of the blind at Jericho. According to Matthew and Mark it was as Jesus was leaving Jericho; according to Luke, as he was entering the town. According to Mark and Luke there was one blind man; according to Matthew, two. All three reports are so evidently based on the same event that it is a desperate expedient to multiply the events. As the narratives stand, they cannot all be exactly true in the same sense. An account of the 'truth' of Scripture has to explain examples such as this. Likewise the frequent discrepancies between Samuel-Kings and Chronicles regarding, for example the size of armies raise the question of what kind of truth is found in these books, and how it is related to the absolute veracity which we ascribe to God.

Examples of the second kind of difficulty are frequent, from the first page of Genesis, where the surface meaning seems to be that light was created before the sun, to the statement in Judith that 'Nabuchodonosor' was king of Nineveh, whereas the real Nebuchadnezzar was king of Babylon. Newman doubtless took this example because Renan had declared 'The book of Judith is a historical impossibility'.[1] Healy's reaction was to take refuge in rigorous literalism, and to appeal to the authority of De Lugo: whether or not the latter would have welcomed the application of his remarks to Nabuchodonosor's being king of Nineveh, Healy interpreted him as saying 'that it is *perfectly clear and evident* that the man who denies it is a heretic'.[2]

In face of such problems for Christian faith in Scripture as God's word, one can deny the problem by abandoning one's belief, or refuse to consider the problem by maintaining a fundamentalist position. For those who are willing to live with the problem, there have been two main lines of approach. The first is to distinguish 'senses' of Scripture: hidden below the apparent surface meaning may be a mysterious deeper meaning which the divine author intended the Christian reader to discover. This process of interpretation, loved by many of the Church Fathers, is freer and more imaginative than the critical art of analysing senses of Scripture which is called Hermeneutics. The object was to help devout readers to find comfort and spiritual nourishment from the whole of Scripture. If the immediate sense appeared untrue, or at variance with another passage, or of no conceivable importance to the message of revelation, or distasteful to piety, or morally discreditable, this was a sign that the eye of faith should look for a deeper sense, to be found usually by treating the surface sense as allegorical. It was Origen who worked out this method, speaking of the 'bodily' sense and the 'spiritual' sense. Some passages, he said, really have no 'bodily' sense: that is, they are not to be taken literally but for their deeper meaning. In this way Origen discusses the imagery of Genesis 1-3

[1] Essay I, § 2, 26, 28: cf. E. Renan, *Recollections of my Youth* (London, 1883), p. 256, and W. Ward, 'Newman and Renan', in *Problems and Persons* (London, 1903) esp. pp. 298-300.

[2] In the second (withheld) article, *Papers and Addresses*, pp. 433-4.

admirably, together with other examples.[1] He solves problems of discrepancy between the Gospels by allegorizing
the narratives,[2] not hesitating even to use such bold expressions as that 'the spiritual truth is often preserved, so to
say, within a historical falsehood'.[3]

Newman speaks of the possible plurality of senses of
Scripture in the 1884 essays,[4] but not as a way of solving
difficulties about the 'truth' of Scripture. In fact Origen's
way has proved a temptation for spiritual writers and has
rendered doubtful service to the cause of exegesis. There
are all too many pages of Ambrose, Augustine and Gregory
where the spiritual doctrine receives no real sanction from
the Scripture passages from which it pretends to be drawn;
it is worth only what it is worth in itself.

Much more fruitful is the second line of approach, which
is to concentrate on the literal sense, understood in its
literary, social and cultural context, and thereby to ascertain what the sacred writer intended to assert, teach or
express: this is the only reliable guide to what God intends,
or primarily intends, to teach us through Scripture. The
method involves the study of the literary forms current in
the author's time, so as to assess what is the literary *genre*
of a book or the form of a passage. The 'truth' we shall look
for will be the kind of 'truth' proper to a given literary
genre, and we must not jump to hasty assumptions about
what this is. Among the Fathers St Augustine and St John
Chrysostom typify this approach. Augustine wrote a whole
work *On the agreement of the Evangelists* to solve difficulties about the truth of Scripture. Both authors point out

---

[1] Origen's theory of inspiration and interpretation is expounded in his
Peri Archon, Book IV. Translation, *Origen on First Principles*, by G. R.
Butterworth (London, 1936), esp. pp. 256-312; on Gen. 1, p. 288.
[2] E.g. *Comm. on St Matthew* XVI, 9-13 (on the blind men at Jericho).
[3] *Comm. on St John* X, 5.
[4] Essay I, § 20.

that the variations in Gospel accounts of the same event argue favourably for their substantial faithfulness: it is exact uniformity which would be suspicious.[1] Both authors say, in the passages referred to, that slighter variations are to be accounted for by the different style of the authors: for more fundamental variations, including omissions and additions, we must seek the cause in the varying intentions of the writers. 'We learn the useful lesson,' says Augustine, 'that nothing else is to be looked for than the speaker's intention' (nihil aliud esse quaerendum quam quid velit qui loquitur);[2] and again,

> From such expressions of the evangelists, different but not contrary, we learn a very useful and most necessary thing: in the words of each we are to look for nothing but the intention (voluntas) which the words ought to serve. Further, that (a writer) is not telling an untruth if he reports in other words someone's meaning without giving his words, to stop wretched nigglers from thinking that truth can be tied, as it were, to the tips of the letters —when in actual fact, not only in words but in all other expressions of meaning, nothing but the meaning itself (ipse animus) should be looked for.[3]

Similarly Chrysostom, in the passage already quoted, says the explanation of differences between the Gospels is to be

---

[1] Augustine, *De Consensu Evangelistarum* II, 12, 28; PL 34, 1091; CSEL XLIII, pp. 127-9. Chrysostom, *Homilies on St Matthew* 1, 2; PG 57, 16-17; translation in *Library of the Fathers* (Oxford, 1843), pp. 4-5; see also J. D. Quinn, 'St John Chrysostom on History in the Synoptics', in CBQ XXIV (1962), pp. 140-7.

[2] *De Cons. Evang.* II, 12, 29; PL 34, 1092; CSEL XLIII, p. 130.

[3] *Ibid.*, II, 28, 67; PL 34, 1111; CSEL XLIII, pp. 171-2. 'Nigglers' renders 'aucupes vocum', 'bird-catchers of words', a favourite figure of Augustine's for pedants who annoyed him.

sought in the varying intentions of the evangelists.[1] In any case, he says, disagreement is on minor points: but

> in matters of capital importance (*en tois kephalaiois*) which sustain our life and weld together our preaching (*kerygma*), nowhere is any of the evangelists to be found in disagreement, not even the slightest.

—And Chrysostom goes on to name such 'capital matters' as the Incarnation, the miracles, the Crucifixion, Resurrection and so on.[2] The might of the Spirit 'prevailed on men, concerned as they were with the more necessary and urgent matters, to take no harm from details'.[3]

The relevance of these passages from the greatest of the Eastern and Western Fathers to Newman's theory of 'obiter dicta' is evident. His 'matters of faith and morals' are precisely Chrysostom's 'capital matters which sustain our life and weld together our preaching'; his 'obiter dicta' are Chrysostom's 'details'. Of course, the Fathers did not say such details were uninspired or could contain error. We have seen how Augustine recoiled from such an idea. Yet he could say quite plainly that they were unimportant, accounted for by merely stylistic variations.

It is in fact stylistic analysis, the study of literary *genres* and forms, which offers the best means of ascertaining the writer's meaning, and distinguishing between the parts of Scripture which are primary, direct expressions of God's revelation in word and in events, and those which are preserved as the background of his action in history—the record of his people's reactions, misunderstandings or failures as well as of his mighty works. Newman's dis-

---

[1] *In Mat.* I, 3; PG. 57, 17-18. Chrysostom uses the words *aitia* (cause, purpose) and *spoudē* (concern) to express the idea of intention.

[2] Ibid., I, 2.

[3] Ibid., I, 3, end.

tinction between the matter of primary concern—'matters of faith and morals', including the historical record of God's action—and things of small importance, though it is a proper distinction to make, was not too happily expressed, and it did not provide as satisfactory an instrument for the analysis of the 'truth' of Scripture as does the study of literary *genres*. It is curious that Newman, with his acute appreciation of the Bible's 'human side, which manifests itself in language, style, tone of thought, character, intellectual peculiarities, and such infirmities, not sinful, as belong to our nature',[1] seems not to have worked out the conclusion that this very variety of expression contains the answer to most apparent problems about the 'truth' of the sacred text. In this he did not go as far as his friend Bishop Clifford, who applied this principle in his *Dublin Review* articles on Genesis I.[2] Clifford argued that the first chapter raises problems only if it is assumed to be in the *genre* of 'history', and to challenge our scientific knowledge of the world: but if we conclude that it is a sort of liturgical hymn in praise of the Creator and celebrating his works within the liturgical framework of the Hebrew seven-day week (as a counterblast to the practice of the neighbouring pagan peoples of dedicating the days of the week to their deities), we have an entirely satisfying account of the passage which makes it perfectly 'true' as a liturgical and didactic poem, and puts it out of range of any charge that it conflicts with scientific truth. In this view of the truth of Genesis 1 Clifford was no innovator: Origen saw that the truth taught in this passage lies deeper than the obviously incorrect account of the order of creation of light and the sun,[3] and Augustine, in a passage which, as we saw, St Thomas quotes, says that

[1] Essay II, § 30.
[2] See above, pp. 25-6, and p. 26, n. 1.
[3] *Peri Archon* IV, 3; Butterworth's translation, p. 288.

it is no business of his whether the sky is like a sphere or a lid, but in order to save people from disbelieving the important teaching of Scripture because of passages which conflict with what they see to be true,

> I must explain briefly, concerning the shape of the sky, that our authors knew the truth about it; but the Spirit of God, who was speaking through them, did not wish to teach men such things as this, which are of no help towards salvation.[1]

Clifford's treatment of Genesis 1, shown by the above examples to be in line with the best patristic interpretation, has a strikingly modern look today, when the Church has at last approved the exegetical principles which make such interpretation entirely acceptable. Newman, as we saw earlier in this Introduction, welcomed Clifford's articles, but did not develop the same line of literary analysis. In fact it was not to become at home in Catholic exegesis until two or three generations later. In between came the Modernist crisis and the official Catholic reaction which, however necessary it may have been, had the unhappy effect of allowing persons of a certain mentality to put forward a Catholic variety of fundamentalism as the only orthodoxy. In this period Newman's unsystematic and somewhat unusually expressed account of inspiration was inevitably misunderstood, misrepresented and prevented from bearing the fruit of the seeds it contained. Today at last we are enjoying that fruit. It is true that the primary debt is now owed to other scholars; Newman's work was the seed that had to fall into the ground and die. But finally, after a process which will be traced briefly in the next section, the Second Vatican Council, in the fullest and most balanced treatment of

---

[1] *De Genesi ad Litteram* II, 9; PL 34, 270-1; CSEL XXVIII, pp. 45-6.

revelation and inspiration yet produced by an ecumenical Council, has defined the scope of inerrancy as 'that truth which God wanted put into the sacred writings for the sake of our salvation'.[1] It is Newman, not Healy or Newman's critics in the period following him, whom the Council has vindicated.

5. Newman's theory and the subsequent development of Catholic doctrine

The scope of this introduction requires some account of the influence that can be ascribed to Newman's theory of inspiration, some discussion of the question how the crisis affecting Catholic biblical studies in the decades following Newman's death was related to his views, and finally an assessment of his position in the light of the eased situation since 1943, and in particular of the teaching of Vatican II. The survey can, however, be fairly summary for the most part, as much of the ground is well covered in accessible books and articles.

Anyone studying the *milieu* of educated English Catholicism in the decades before the Modernist crisis must be struck by its intellectual vigour and mature confidence, not paralysed by the fear that any display of sincere and inquiring reflection would bring charges of disloyalty. Newman was not alone in his confident view that the 'conflict' of the Bible with modern science was a problem for Protestantism rather than for Catholicism. Not all, doubtless, could have shared the dispassionate calm of one of his notes weighing Darwin's theory of evolution against the consequences of denying it:

[1] *Const. De divina Revelatione* III, § 11. The whole passage is quoted and discussed below.

I will either go whole hog with Darwin, or, dispensing with time and history altogether, hold, not only the theory of distinct species but that also of the creation of fossil-bearing rocks;[1]

nevertheless, the leadership enjoyed by the English Catholics was such that *The Descent of Man* had to wait only a few months for a serious and fair-minded discussion, together with three other weighty works, by a Bishop (Hedley).[2] The quality of Bishop Clifford's essays on the Genesis creation account has been referred to above. The relaxed attitude among intelligent lay Catholics is typified by a delightful story told by Mivart in one of the first of his ill-fated series of articles in *The Nineteenth Century*.

I well recollect dining at a priest's house (in or about 1870), when one of the party, the late accomplished Mr Richard Simpson of Clapham (a most pious Catholic and weekly communicant), expressed some ordinary scientific views on the subject of the deluge. A startled auditor asked anxiously, 'But is not, then, the account in the Bible of the deluge true?' To which Mr Simpson replied, 'True! Of course it is true. There was a local inundation, and some of the sacerdotal caste saved themselves in a punt, with their cocks and hens.'[3]

But this theological freedom was not based on clear enough principles: even Newman's thought on inspiration illustrates this, at least as regards the working-out of his principles. From our vantage-point of today, with the distinctions that have been developed in the theology of

[1] BOA, A.46.3, Book of Sundries, p. 83, 9 Dec 1863.

[2] Cf. 'Evolution and Faith', in *The Dublin Review*, New Series, XVII (1871), pp. 1-40 (reprinted in Bishop Hedley, *Evolution and Faith, with other essays*, London 1931).

[3] Cf. St George Mivart, 'The Catholic Church and Biblical Criticism' in *The Nineteenth Century* XXII (1887), p. 49, footnote 22.

revelation and inspiration, we can both acknowledge his
orthodoxy and appreciate his concern for lawful freedom;
but in the latter decades of the nineteenth century the relationship of science to faith was a more painful question, as
is illustrated by the life of Dr St George Mivart.[1] This
eminent biologist, who had become a Catholic in 1844 at
the age of 17, in his later years made increasingly strong
claims for the autonomy of science in relation to the
Church's teaching authority, especially in a series of articles
in *The Nineteenth Century* from 1885 to January, 1900. Particularly on account of his views on hell, he came into conflict with his former friend, Cardinal Vaughan, who treated
him with great rigour and finally excommunicated him, in
which condition he died in April, 1900.

Mivart's trouble, as Wilfrid Ward showed, was that from
one side or the other he never grasped the true principle of
the development of doctrine.[2] On inspiration, he understood
Newman to have rendered tenable the view that only parts
of the Bible are inspired, and that 'principles are already
freely admitted which are amply sufficient to insure our
complete scientific freedom in this matter'.[3] By 1900 Mivart
was openly saying that the doctrine of inerrancy had been
explained away till it meant nothing.[4]

Much more serious and widespread was the theological
unrest on the Continent, with which Newman's name was
to be unjustly linked by some later critics. A good survey
of the situation is available to English readers in Jean Levie's

[1] Cf. Jacob W. Gruber, *A Conscience in Conflict: The Life of St
George Jackson Mivart* (New York, 1960).
[2] Cf. W. Ward, 'Unchanging Dogma and Changeful Man', in *Problems and Persons* (London, 1903), pp. 99-132.
[3] *The Nineteenth Century*, XXII (1887), pp. 47-9.
[4] 'The Continuity of Catholicism', in *The Nineteenth Century*, XLVII
(1900), pp. 51-72, esp. pp. 58-62. It was this article and another, 'Some
Recent Apologists', published simultaneously in *The Fortnightly Review*,
which caused Mivart's excommunication by Cardinal Vaughan.

The Bible, Word of God in Words of Men,[1] while the crisis
in France which evoked the encyclical *Providentissimus
Deus* in 1893, and the question whether Newman's theory
was envisaged, has been outlined by H. J. T. Johnson.[2] There
were three tendencies which have been labelled 'l'école
large', 'l'école étroite' and 'l'école moyenne'; they were not
schools in the proper sense, but the classes into which biblical scholars in the 1880's and 90's fell with respect to their
views on the extent of inspiration and inerrancy. The first
class, who tended to qualify or restrict inspiration and inerrancy, may be held to include the German A. Rohling,
who resurrected the view of Holden;[3] the Sicilian Canon
S. di Bartolo, who proposed a subtle theory of varying
degrees of inspiration in different categories of subject-
matter in the Bible;[4] F. Lenormant, who suggested that
inspiration is restricted to matters of faith and morals,
expounding his view more uncompromisingly than Newman,[5] and the young Loisy, who was already causing great
anxiety in the 1880's when he was being groomed for a chair
of Scripture at the Institut Catholique of Paris. Naturally

[1] *La Bible, parole humaine et message de Dieu*, Paris-Louvain, 1958;
Eng. tr., London 1961; see ch. 3, 'Trends in Catholic exegesis, 1880-1914'
and ch. 4, 'Religious authority and the biblical movement, 1890-1914'.
[2] 'Leo XIII, Cardinal Newman and the Inerrancy of Scripture', in
The Downside Review LXIX (1951), pp. 411-27. For fuller accounts see
E. Mangenot, art. 'Inspiration de l'Écriture', in *Dictionnaire de Théologie
Catholique* VII, cols. 2187-92, and V. Larranaga, 'En el cincuentenario de
la Encíclica "Providentissimus Deus"', in *Estudios Biblicos* III (1944),
pp. 3-24;—'La Crisis bíblica en el Instituto Católico de Paris (1881-93),
ibid., pp. 173-88, 383-96.
[3] 'Die Inspiration der Bibel und ihre Bedeutung für die freie For-
schung', in *Natur und Offenbarung* (Münster, 1872).
[4] *I Criteri teologici: la storia dei dommi e la libertà delle affermazioni*
(Turin, 1888), published with judicious revisions as *Les critères théo-
logiques* (Paris, 1889), but put on the Index in 1891; the Rome edition
of 1904 was, however, approved.
[5] *Les origines de l'histoire d'après la Bible et les traditions de peuples
orientaux* (ed. 2, Paris, 1880), put on the Index in 1887.

the scholars of this first tendency welcomed Newman's
articles, and no one can be blamed for associating Newman
with this class on a basis of theological position, however far
he stood from a Loisy.

It is observable that the scholars of 'l'école large' were
men who were directly concerned with the most difficult
sector of the debate between Catholic and non-Catholic
biblical studies—the point where the findings of archaeology
and the sciences had to be related to the traditional understanding of biblical history. The scholars on the opposing
side were not always so directly concerned, though the
Sulpician Abbé F. Vigouroux, often represented as the
leader of 'l'école étroite', deserves well of posterity as the
founder of the *Dictionnaire de la Bible*. It was those who,
like the Abbé De Broglie, tried to maintain a middle course,
satisfying the demands of Catholic Tradition and growing
knowledge, of loyalty and intellectual integrity, who
were to see the Church through. They were to find their
greatest representative in the young Dominican M. J.
Lagrange, who founded the École pratique d'études
bibliques at Jerusalem in 1890.[1]

But in France things had to get worse before they could
get better. At the centre was that noble figure, Mgr Maurice
d'Hulst, Rector of the Paris Institut Catholique, a follower
of the Good Shepherd not in the pleasant meadows of parochial life but in the pitiless jungle of academic scholarship.[2]
His troubles came from his intellectual integrity, his concern for true biblical scholarship, and his rare loyalty to a
subordinate who let him down. Criticized first for the
charitable tone of an article on the death of Renan in 1892,
he ran into worse trouble three months later when he

[1] Cf. J. Levie, *The Bible, Word of God in Words of Men*, p. 44 and
bibliography there.
[2] Cf. Cardinal Baudrillart, *Vie de Mgr d'Hulst* (Paris, 1914).

published a famous article, 'La question biblique' in *Le Correspondant* of 25 January, 1893.[1] In this article he characterized the various tendencies in contemporary Catholic biblical scholarship, and described the sort of view current among 'l'école large', as holding that the whole Bible is inspired but revelation is not present everywhere: divine truth is only concerned with revelation, concerning matters of faith and morals, and inerrancy is limited to this field. D'Hulst wrote with sympathy but not as one putting forward his own view.

The article immediately touched off a controversy in the pages of *Études religieuses* and *Science Catholique*, in the course of which the latter journal also published a critical discussion of Newman's theory, 'Ya-t-il dans la Bible des propositions non inspirées?' by the Belgian Jesuit J. Corluy.[2] In November appeared the encyclical of Pope Leo XIII, *Providentissimus Deus*. Though it got a poor press among non-Catholic biblical scholars,[3] it should be appreciated that for all its cautiousness its aim was to encourage and foster sound biblical studies such as were flourishing under Père Lagrange's guidance: the encyclical should not be read in the light of the papal documents against Modernism over ten years later.[4] However, the Pope included an explicit censure of those who proposed to limit inspiration to matters of faith and morals. He allowed that sometimes manuscript readings might be faulty, and the correct reading might sometimes remain doubtful, in which case scholars must proceed by the rules of sound criticism;

[1] Cf. H. J. T. Johnson, *The Downside Review* LXIX (1951), pp. 411-13; E. Mangenot in DTC VII, 2188-9, and V. Larrañaga (art. cit. on p. 82, n. 2 who, however, is unsympathetic to d'Hulst.
[2] *Science Catholique*, May 1893, pp. 481-507.
[3] Cf. H. J. T. Johnson, *The Downside Review* LXIX (1951), pp. 414-15.
[4] Cf. J. Levie, *The Bible, Word of God . . .* , pp. 61-7.

but it would be entirely unlawful either to restrict inspiration to certain parts only of Scripture, or to admit
that the sacred author himself had erred. We cannot
tolerate the position of those who free themselves from
these difficulties by daring to concede that divine inspiration belongs to matters of faith and morals and nothing
beyond, because they mistakenly think that, in questions
of the truth of a passage, it is less important to discover
what God said than to consider *why* He said it.

For all the books which the Church receives as sacred
and canonical, with all their parts, are wholly and entirely
written at the dictation of the Holy Spirit; not only can
no error coexist (subesse) with divine inspiration, but the
latter absolutely excludes all error, and that with the
same necessity whereby God, the supreme Truth, cannot
be the author of any error.[1]

Mgr d'Hulst took himself to be censured and at once
submitted whole-heartedly. There is no doubt that it was
the French situation which the Pope had in mind, and no
evidence that Newman's articles were directly envisaged;[2]
it was possible for a sympathetic interpreter such as Fr
Vincent McNabb to represent Newman's true meaning in
an entirely orthodox light,[3] but it is useless to deny that
Newman had used the language of 'restriction to matters
of faith and morals', and in a period of crisis no one can be
blamed if Newman's theory was held to fall under the
general censure. If, however, any distress was able to
reach him in heaven, St Augustine and St Thomas will

[1] Denz. 1950-1 [3291-2].
[2] Cf. H. J. T. Johnson, art. cit., pp. 415 ff.
[3] 'Cardinal Newman and the Inspiration of Scripture', in *Where
Believers May Doubt* (London, 1903), pp. 31-50.

have been at hand with ready assurances of understanding.

Of the Modernist crisis itself there is little need to say much here. Some of the Modernists may have appealed to Newman, but it was clear enough that if they had rightly understood his theory of the development of doctrine they would not be where they were.[1] What can be said with relevance to Newman's theory of inspiration is that the general impression which it had created prevented the seminal ideas it contained from developing and bearing fruit throughout the period that was overshadowed by the fear of Modernism. Newman's theory appeared next to Holden's among unsound views in the Fundamental Theology manuals, and articles on him as late as 1938 (J. Duggan) and 1944 (A. Larrañaga) commended Healy's replies more than Newman's articles,[2] neither of these authors either approaching the sympathy of Vincent Mc-Nabb, nor discerning the unfairness and irrelevance of many of Healy's points. During this period seminary theology, especially in Italy, was preoccupied with defending the propositions of the Catholic faith against anything that savoured of Modernism. The product of this mentality in the field of biblical studies was a kind of fundamentalism. Its representatives saw nothing but danger in the labours of those excellent and loyal Catholic scholars, especially in the Dominican Biblical School and the Pontifical Biblical Institute run by the Jesuits, all of whose exegetical and archaeological studies were leading them more and more to see that the solution to many problems concerning the 'truth' of Scripture was to be found through the analysis

---

[1] Cf. E. O'Dwyer, Bishop of Limerick, *Cardinal Newman and the Encyclical 'Pascendi'* (London, 1908).

[2] J. Duggan, 'Num sententia Cardinalis Newman de inerrantia Sacrae Scripturae defendi possit?' (directly against McNabb), in *Verbum Domini* 18 (1938), pp. 219-24; A. Larrañaga, in *Estudios Biblicos* III (1944), pp. 13-24.

of literary *genres*. A discreditable publication by an Italian priest in 1941 occasioned a reply by the Pontifical Biblical Commission (a very conservative body, but one which had always exercised a genuine concern for sound scholarship) and, in 1943, the encyclical which is still considered the Magna Carta of modern Catholic biblical studies, *Divino Afflante Spiritu*.[1]

This encyclical marks a turning-point in the fortunes of serious biblical scholarship in the Catholic Church; it was the sign that the Roman authorities were prepared to trust the scholars more fully, and from now on it was the Biblical Commission itself which gave cautious encouragement to the exercise of a greater exegetical freedom,[2] and defended the scholars against the constant sniping campaign, pursued with sadly little concern for truth or justice, by the Italian fundamentalists. The latter showed a curious inconsistency in their otherwise exaggeratedly papalist ecclesiology, in that they could never stomach *Divino Afflante Spiritu*. In the years immediately preceding the second Vatican Council and during its first two years their attacks on the Pontifical Biblical Institute formed one of the most disedifying episodes in modern Church history.[3] The relevance of these disturbances to our present theme

[1] The encyclical is published by the C.T.S. as *Stand by the Bible*. For background and summary, cf. J. Levie, *The Bible, Word of God . . .* , ch. 7. The whole second part of this work presents a view of inspiration which develops the guiding lines in the encyclical.

[2] See the documents of 1955 quoted by J. Levie, op. cit., pp. 186-90.

[3] The lamentable story is summarized by 'Xavier Rynne' in *Letters from Vatican City* (London, 1962), pp. 52-6. The present writer was in Rome during this period, saw copies of most of the relevant public and private documents, and vouches for the truth of 'Xavier Rynne's' account. The libellous article in *Divinitas* 4 (1960), pp. 387-456 was answered, with quiet dignity and nothing like the same publicity, by the faculty of the Pontifical Biblical Institute in *Verbum Domini* 39 (1961), pp. 3-17. The unjust suspension of Fathers Lyonnet and Zerwick, without charges, sentence or defence, continued till 1965, when it was quietly ended without apology or amends.

is that the focus of anxiety was precisely the 'truth' of Scripture, and it was the Italian fundamentalists themselves who forced the pace towards the clarification achieved by the second Vatican Council.

That the crisis was largely in the minds of the fundamentalists is shown by the tone of the document which the Biblical Commission issued in 1964 to give guidance.[1] It is an encouragement to the scholarly and responsible use of the methods of exegesis and hermeneutics employed in sound Scripture studies today, especially the study of literary *genres* and the cultural milieu of the Old and New Testaments, and including the technique of Form Criticism; it contains only moderately-worded warnings against the danger of underemphasizing the historical truth of the Gospels,[2] and against giving general publicity to the private speculations of scholars.

Meanwhile the Second Vatican Council, among its dogmatic concerns, was engaged on the formulation of a document on revelation, dealing with the themes of Scripture and Tradition,[3] of inspiration, and of the interpretation of the Old and the New Testament. This is not the place to recount the story of the rejection in 1962 of the first schema with its too rigid disjunction between Scripture and Tradition, or of the gradual development of the final *Constitution on Revelation* up to its promulgation in November, 1965. For our purposes it will suffice to quote from and comment on Ch. III, 'Concerning the divine

---

[1] *Instruction concerning the historical truth of the Gospels*, 14 May 1964; *Acta Apostolicae Sedis* 56 (1964) pp. 712-18. Translation in Cardinal A. Bea, *The Study of the Synoptic Gospels* (London, 1965), pp. 79-89.

[2] This repeated a brief and equally moderate 'monitum' issued by the Holy Office in 1961 (A.A.S. 53 [1961], p. 507).

[3] Cf. 'Xavier Rynne', *Letters from Vatican City*, ch. V, 'The Debate on the Sources of Revelation', pp. 140-73.

Inspiration of Sacred Scripture, and its Interpretation'.

The chapter begins with a re-affirmation of what had already been declared about revelation and God's authorship at Vatican I. Then follows the further explanation of the relationship of the human author to the divine author, as we have quoted it above (p. 60). The next paragraph deals with the 'truth' of Scripture and must be quoted in full:

Cum ergo omne id, quod auctores inspirati seu hagiographi asserunt, retineri debeat assertum a Spiritu Sancto, inde Scripturae libri veritatem, quam Deus nostrae salutis causa Litteris Sacris consignari voluit, firmiter, fideliter et sine errore docere profitendi sunt.

Since everything asserted by the inspired authors or sacred writers must be held to be asserted by the Holy Spirit, it follows that the books of Scripture must be acknowledged as teaching firmly, faithfully and without error that truth which God wanted put into the sacred writings for the sake of our salvation.

There follows, in explanation, a quotation of 2 Tim. 3:16-17, which likewise expresses the purpose of inspired Scripture. The appended note refers to the passages from St Thomas and St Augustine which we have already considered, as well as to Trent, Vatican I and the encyclical *Divino Afflante Spiritu.*

It is evident that this paragraph makes a notable contribution to the problem we have traced through doctrinal history and in the case of Newman—namely, how to speak satisfactorily about the 'truth' of Scripture without either asserting too little and admitting error, or asserting too much and running into difficulties of explaining passages in Scripture which clash with truths known from other sources. The 'truth' of Scripture is *defined* with relation to its purpose, but not *restricted* in its material extent. The key sentence thus avoids any hint of the impression Newman unfortunately gave, while expressing with admirable clarity what he was trying to emphasize.

Before commenting on this paragraph in greater detail, we may briefly survey the rest of the chapter. If the 'message' of Scripture is related to God's purpose of our salvation and does not necessarily involve every proposition in Scripture (or at least not equally) it is all-important to find and interpret *what God is teaching us*. The method is that commended in *Divino Afflante Spiritu* and the 1964 *Instruction*: seek the intention of the human writer, and the key to that will be found through the study of literary *genres*. A correct method here will free the interpreter at the start from the sort of misunderstandings which, apparently, destroyed the young Renan's faith. When, for example, by study of the *genre* of *midrash haggadah* we realize that the book of Judith is an early example of it, Nabuchodonosor can be left in peace at last, and we can begin to assess the very simple and general message of encouragement to faithfulness in persecution which the author intended.

But the study of literary *genres* is not the whole of exegesis, nor does it take us all the way. We read the Bible as Christians and our interpretation depends on theological principles, which we must apply after our *literary* assessment: these are stated with admirable clarity in the chapter we are studying. The first is the purpose of revelation and the scope of divine truth contained in Scripture: it is that truth which God wanted expressed 'for the sake of our salvation'. That truth, we know as Christians, is Christ: what we listen for in Scripture is Christ's voice. This leads us to the second principle: revelation is progressive, and an earlier text must be read by Christians in the light of the full revelation given in Christ. 'We must attend to the content and unity of the whole of Scripture, taking into account the living tradition of the whole Church and the analogy of faith.' The Old Testament contains the earlier stages of revelation: some of them magnificent, some of them, like Judith, impressing us by their incomplete character in comparison with the fulness of light in the New Testament.[1]

To return to the paragraph on the 'truth' of Scripture, we may learn more about its exact sense by study of the stages through which the text was developed. Originally the term 'inerrancy' was used: it was dropped in favour of the more traditional, positive word 'truth'. The word 'inerrancy' (which Newman did not use) leads too easily to a false statement of the questions at issue, and the notion of 'truth' which it has presupposed in recent times, has too often been a more modern and quasi-philosophical one than the biblical idea.[2] Further, there was a development from an insistence on the material extent of inerrancy as concerning every kind of proposition in Scripture, towards a definition of the scope of divine truth, involving the exclusion of error with respect to that scope. Thus the rejected first schema, in a sentence only slightly rephrased from *Providentissimus Deus*, said that 'Inspiration excludes

[1] Cf. the valuable commentary by I. de la Potterie, 'La vérité de la Sainte Écriture et L'Histoire du Salut d'après la Constitution dogmatique "Dei Verbum"', in *Nouvelle Revue Théologique* 88 (1966), pp. 149-69. He considers the definition of the scope of divine truth in Scripture given by the Council to have been most nearly approached by P. Grelot in *La Bible Parole de Dieu* (Paris-Tournai, 1965), pp. 96-134; Grelot defines the object of revelation as 'le mystère du salut réalisé dans le Christ'. On the progressive character of revelation he refers to the brilliant but controversial article by N. Lohfink, 'Über die Irrtumslosigkeit und die Einheit der Schrift', in *Stimmen der Zeit* 174 (1963-4), pp. 161-81 (summary in *Theology Digest* XIII [1965], pp. 185-92).

[2] Cf. I. de la Potterie, art. cit., pp. 153-4.

D

all error in every matter, religious or profane'.[1] The first
draft of the new schema said that 'the entire books of
Scripture with all their parts must be acknowledged to
teach truth without any error'. The revised draft (1964)
qualified 'truth' for the first time, with the adjective '*salutaris*', 'related to salvation', and added a string of adverbs,
'unshakeably, faithfully and entirely' before 'without any
error'.[2] In the final text the words 'entire with all their
parts' were moved to a position in the first sentence on
inspiration, the adverbs were reduced to avoid unnecessary
repetitions and, most important of all, '*salutarem*' was
changed to the longer qualification 'which God wanted put
into the sacred writings for the sake of our salvation'. 184
bishops had asked for '*salutarem*' to be omitted, 'because,
contrary to the documents of the Magisterium, it seems to
restrict inerrancy to matters of faith and morals'. Others
wanted the word kept, with a reference to St Augustine;
others wanted it replaced by various alternatives. The drafting committee, while defending 'salutarem', accepted the
alternative proposed by 73 bishops which now stands in
the text.[3] It is generally agreed that the text as finally
promulgated is a most satisfying conclusion to a long
debate. It represents the mind of St Augustine and St
Thomas (referred to in the official notes) and it marks the
end of the century-long scare about inerrancy. It means
that fundamentalism is not Catholic orthodoxy, and, with
regard to the theme of this essay, it vindicates what Newman, clearly if somewhat gropingly, was trying to say.

It has been said that Vatican I was Manning's Council,
the Church not being ready for Newman, but that Vatican
II is Newman's. This is an exaggeration if one looks for

[1] First schema (Vatican, 1962), p. 13.
[2] Revised schema (Vatican, 1964), p. 21.
[3] *Modi* issued on 20 Oct 1965, pp. 33-4. On this development cf.
'Xavier Rynne', *The Fourth Session* (London, 1966), pp. 189-92.

explicit reference to him in the Council documents; I do not know of any. Newman was often mentioned in Council speeches, and some bishops wanted his name, as well as that of Teilhard de Chardin, mentioned in the Constitution *On the Church in the Modern World*,[1] but they are not named explicitly. If, however, we look for a more general influence of Newman on the Council we find it both in broad lines and in details, both in theological trends and in practical developments. To start with particular points, the passages of the Constitution *On Divine Revelation* examined above will be accepted by any fair-minded reader of Newman today as expressing what he was trying to say. The idea, so dear to Newman and expressed in the first 1884 article, that Scripture is a kind of sacrament, the food of the soul as truly as the Eucharist, is expressed in Chapter VI of the *Constitution on Divine Revelation*:

The Church has always venerated the divine Scriptures just as she venerates the body of the Lord, since from the table of both the word of God and of the body of Christ she unceasingly receives and offers to the faithful the bread of life, especially in the sacred liturgy.[2]

The propriety of 'consulting the faithful', for drawing attention to which Newman suffered so much,[3] has been accepted (after a very stuffy beginning) not only in practice

---

[1] Cf. 'Xavier Rynne', *The Third Session* (London, 1965), p. 126.
[2] *Revelation* VI, 21; cf. ibid., 26 and *Liturgy* II, 51, echoing the *Imitation of Christ*, IV, 11, 4. It is characteristic of the consistent clash of mentalities in the Council that some of the so-called 'conservatives' fought against the use of this eminently traditional and Augustinian language because they smelt danger to their idea of the Eucharist (cf. *Modi* on Revelation issued on 20 Oct 1965, p. 60).
[3] Cf. *On Consulting the Faithful in Matters of Doctrine*, ed. John Coulson (London, 1961).

but also in the permanent documents of the Council.[1] This is only one aspect of the constant emphasis on 'dialogue' which the Council, faithful to Pope John's intention, has maintained, and thereby has also come closer to the spirit of Newman.

More broadly, the constant divergence of theological attitudes in the Council makes one think of Newman, and thereby to see that it is Newman's attitude which has been accepted by the voice of the Council. The use of political terms such as 'conservative' and 'progressive' is to be deplored. The confrontation has been much better expressed as being between 'defenders of a non-historical orthodoxy' and those who have a truly historical vision of God's work in and for the world. Perhaps no theologian since the age of the Fathers has illumined our understanding of God's work in history so much as Newman. This light plays on the first two chapters of the *Constitution on the Church*, which boldly turn from the static and institutionalizing tendency of the 'anti-Modernist' period to a view of the 'Pilgrim Church' which owes much to Newman's ideas. Chapter II of the *Constitution on Divine Revelation* depends even more clearly on Newman's idea of 'development'.

Finally—and to return to a theme which is central to the essays republished here—the second Vatican Council has constantly expressed its intention of not adding to dogmatic definitions, and of leaving open controverted questions in order to concentrate on pastoral concerns. In this the Council has exemplified that spirit for which Newman fought and suffered. The contrary mentality, repre-

---

[1] E.g. *On the Church* II, 12 (the basic idea of the universal *sensus fidei*); the need for the clergy to consult and listen to the laity is stated in *On the Church* IV, 37; *On the Ministry and Life of Priests* II, 9; cf. *On the Pastoral Duties of Bishops* I, 13; *On the Church in the Modern World* II, 3, 62, etc.

sented in Newman's day by Healy and by all too many in dominant positions since him, tends to see theological progress in terms of the solution of questions, which then leave ever-decreasing room for free debate. Yet Trent, for all its concern to defend Catholic truth against the Reformers, severely limited its scope and, as the *acta* show, constantly avoided prejudicing questions debated between Catholics, or even (in the case of divorce) between Catholics and Orthodox.[1] While it must be admitted that a concern not to decide questions was less dominant at Vatican I, it has been apparent again and again (here also in faithfulness to Pope John's intention) at Vatican II, as the *relationes* of the drafting commissions show. Examples are the extraordinary care given to the formulation of the relationship between Scripture and Tradition,[2] the avoidance of the question whether only bishops can ordain priests,[3] a number of notes saying that certain biblical texts are not adduced in order not to prejudice debates between exegetes,[4] and the careful disavowal which accompanies the application of the title 'Mediatrix' to Our Lady.[5]

During the third session of Vatican II, Father Dominic Barberi, the Passionist who received Newman into the Catholic Church at Littlemore in 1845, was beatified. Pope Paul VI in his sermon on the occasion dwelt so forcibly on Newman himself that one theologian remarked to the present writer 'you would almost think it was Newman he

---

[1] Cf. H. Lennerz, 'Das Konzil von Trient und theologische Schulmeinungen', in *Scholastik* IV (1929), pp. 38-53; M. Bévenot, ' "Faith and Morals" in the Councils of Trent and Vatican I', in *The Heythrop Journal* III (1962), p. 23.

[2] *Revelation* II, 9: cf. *Modi* of 20 Oct 1965, pp. 72-3.

[3] *On the Church* III, 21; cf. Schema of 1964, p. 87.

[4] E.g. on the seven 'deacons' in Acts 6, *Church* III, 29 1964 Schema, p. 104.

[5] *On the Church* VIII, 62; 1964 Schema, p 214.

was beatifying'. The Pope, changing into English for the conclusion of his sermon, described Newman as

> him who, in full consciousness of his mission—'I have a work to do'—and guided solely by love of the truth and fidelity to Christ, traced an itinerary, the most toilsome, but also the greatest, the most meaningful, the most conclusive, that human thought ever travelled during the last century, indeed one might say during the modern era, to arrive at the fulness of wisdom and of peace.[1]

---

[1] Sermon on 27 Oct 1963, A.A.S. 55 (1963), p. 1025. Immediately below, the Pope describes Newman as 'so high an authority of a time like ours'.

NOTE ON THE PRESENTATION OF THE TEXT

The basic text printed here is that found in *Stray Essays*, which is the final form of both of Newman's 1884 articles. The first essay has been compared with the original privately-printed pamphlet, corrected by Newman but without the emendations suggested by correspondents, and with the article as published in *The Nineteenth Century*. The second essay has been compared with the pamphlet Newman published in reply to Healy's attack. All the versions compared are those considered by Newman as ready for publication at each distinct stage of the project. This is clearly more desirable than an attempt to compare the final versions with the early drafts or copies which remain; but in order to see the development of the articles the following list in chronological order, with the necessary references to the Birmingham Oratory Archives, has been prepared.

Essay I

1. Extant draft and copy in Newman's hand (A.35.1 and A.32.5), and in Neville's hand with Newman's corrections (A.38.5).
2. Various printings and proofs of the pamphlet 'On the Inspiration of Scripture', both without the final note on 'Auctor utriusque Testamenti' and then including the note, with other corrections by Newman (A.35.1).
3. A copy of the pamphlet on which Newman wrote 'State of the text as sent to the Revisers for remark with note as

the end' (A. 13.2). (*This was the copy used for comparison.*) (*Siglum* A)

4. Copy corrected for publication (A. 35.1).
5. The article 'On the Inspiration of Scripture' which appeared in *The Nineteenth Century*, No. 84 (February, 1884), pp. 185-99. (*Siglum* B)
6. *Stray Essays on controversial points variously illustrated:* by Cardinal Newman. 1890. Privately printed.

Essay II
1. Draft in Neville's hand with Newman's corrections (A.45.1).
2. Printed versions of 'Postscript' corrected (A.32.9).
3. The pamphlet 'What is of obligation for a Catholic to believe concerning the Inspiration of the Canonical Scriptures, being a postscript to an article in the February No. of the "Nineteenth Century Review", in answer to Professor Healy, by Cardinal Newman'. London, 1884. (*Siglum* C)
4. 'Postscript' reprinted and corrected for *Stray Essays* (A.40.8).
5. *Stray Essays.*

Thus the variants referred to by A and B are in the earlier stages of Essay I (nos. 3 and 5); those referred to by C, in the first form of Essay II (no. 3). (The footnotes with asterisks are Newman's own.) While even the smallest verbal discrepancy has been noted, it has not been thought necessary to record mere changes in punctuation—including the use of capitals or brackets, paragraphs, italics, abbreviations or the style of scripture references—where the words and sense remained the same. Also certain small points of typographical style have been regularized in accordance with good modern practice.

PART TWO

THE TEXT

ESSAY I

INSPIRATION IN ITS RELATION TO REVELATION[1]

§ 1.

It has lately been asked, what answer do we Catholics give to the allegation urged against us by men of the day, to the effect that we demand of our converts an assent to views and interpretations of Scripture which modern science and historical research have utterly discredited.

As this alleged obligation is confidently maintained against us, and with an array of instances in support of it, I think it should be either denied or defended; and the best mode perhaps of doing, whether the one or the other, will be, instead of merely dealing with the particular instances adduced in proof, to state what we really do hold as regards Holy Scripture, and what a Catholic is bound to believe. This I propose now to do, and in doing it, I beg it to be understood that my statements are simply my own, and involve no responsibility of any one besides myself.

§ 2.

A recent work of M. Renan's is one of those publications which have suggested or occasioned this adverse criticism upon our intellectual position. That author's abandonment of Catholicism seems (according to a late article in a journal of high reputation) in no small measure to have come about by his study of the Biblical text, especially that of the Old Testament. 'He explains,' says the article, 'that

[1] AB, 'ON THE INSPIRATION OF SCRIPTURE'.

the Roman Catholic Church admits no compromise on questions of Biblical criticism and history' . . . even though[1] 'the Book of Judith is an historical impossibility. Hence the undoubted fact that the Roman Catholic Church . . . insists on its members believing . . . a great deal more in pure criticism and pure history than the strictest Protestants exact from their pupils or flocks.' Should, then, a doubting Anglican contemplate becoming Catholic by way of attaining intellectual peace, 'if his doubts turn on history and criticism, he will find the little finger of the Catholic Church thicker than the loins of Protestantism'.

§ 3.

The serious question, then, which this article calls on us to consider, is, whether it is 'an undoubted fact', as therein stated, that the Catholic Church does 'insist' on her children's acceptance of certain Scripture informations on matters of fact in defiance of criticism and history. And my first duty on setting out is to determine the meaning of that vague word 'insists', which I shall use in the only sense in which a Catholic can consent to use it.

I allow, then, that the Church, certainly, does 'insist', when she speaks dogmatically, nay, or rather she more than insists, she obliges; she obliges us to an internal assent to that which she proposes to us. So far I admit, or rather maintain. And I admit that she obliges us in a most forcible and effective manner, that is, by the penalty of forfeiting communion with her, if we refuse our internal assent to her word. We cannot be real Catholics, if we do not from our heart accept the matters which she puts forward as divine and true. This is plain.

---

[1] 'Even though': A, 'Thus': B, 'though'

§ 4

Next, to what does the Church oblige us? and what is her warrant for doing so? I answer: The matters which she can oblige us to accept with an internal assent are the matters contained in that Revelation of Truth,[1] written or unwritten, which came to the world from our Lord and His Apostles; and this claim on our faith in her decisions as to the matter of that Revelation rests on her being the divinely-appointed representative of the Apostles, and the expounder of their words; so that whatever she categorically delivers about their formal acts, or their writings or their teaching, is an Apostolic deliverance. I repeat, the only sense in which the Church 'insists' on any statement, Biblical or other, the only reason of her so insisting, is that that statement is part of the original Revelation, and therefore must be unconditionally accepted,—else, that Revelation is not, as a revelation, accepted at all.

The question then which I have to answer is: *What*, in matter of fact, has the Church (or the Pope), as the representative of God, said about Scripture, which, as being Apostolic, unerring Truth,[2] is obligatory on our faith—that is, is *de fide*?

§ 5.

Many truths may be predicated about Scripture and its contents which are not obligatory on our faith, viz., such as are private conclusions from premises, or are the *dicta* of theologians: such as about the author of the Book of Job, or the dates of St Paul's Epistles. These are not obligatory upon us, because they are not the subjects of

[1] 'Of Truth': not in A.
[2] A added: 'or what is called dogma'.

ex cathedrâ utterances of a General Council.[1] Opinions of this sort may be true or not true, and lie open for acceptance or rejection, since no divine utterance has ever been granted to us about them, or is likely to be granted. We are not bound to believe what St Jerome said or inferred about Scripture; nor[2] what St Augustine, or St Thomas, or Cardinal Caietan, or Fr Perrone has said; but what the Church has enunciated, what the Councils, what the Pope, has determined. We are not bound to accept with an absolute faith what[3] is not an Ecumenical dogma, or the equivalent of dogma (*vide infra*, § 17), that is, what is not *de fide*; such judgments, however powerfully enunciated,[4] we may without loss of communion doubt, we may refuse to accept. This is what we must especially bear in mind, when we handle such objections as M. Renan's. We must not confuse what is indisputable as well as true, with what may indeed be true, yet is disputable. And[5] this is to be received, not only as against M. Renan, but as against such criticisms as are to be met with in the publications of the day.[5]

§ 6.[6]

I must make one concession to him. In certain cases there may be a duty of silence, when there is no obligation of belief. Here no question of faith comes in. We will sup-

---

[1] 'A General Council': AB, 'the Church'.

[2] A, 'not'.

[3] A, 'what is not a dogma, what is not *de fide*'.

[4] 'However powerfully enunciated': AB, 'however high their authority'.

[5-5] Not in A or B.

[6] In A § 6 reads: 'But I have here a limitation, or at least a caution, to introduce. It is possible, as I have been implying, that a novel opinion about Scripture or its portions may be true, and an old opinion erroneous, in a case where the Church has hitherto decided nothing about them, and a new question requires a new answer. It is permissible, because it is not against the faith. However, we should be very certain of its truth, and of its effect upon others, before we can feel that its abstract per-

pose that a novel opinion about Scripture or its contents is well grounded, and that a received opinion is open to doubt,[1] in a case in which the Church has hitherto decided nothing, so that a new question needs a new answer: here, to profess the new opinion may be abstractedly permissible, but is not always permissible in practice. The novelty may be so startling as to require a full certainty that it is true; it may be so strange as to raise the question whether it will not unsettle ill-educated minds,—that is, though the statement is not an offence against faith, still it may be an offence against charity. It need not be heretical, yet at a particular time or place it may be so contrary to the prevalent opinion in the Catholic body, as in Galileo's case, that zeal for the supremacy of the Divine Word, deference to existing authorities, charity towards the weak and ignorant, and distrust of self, should keep a man from being impetuous or careless in circulating what nevertheless he holds to be true, and what, if indeed asked about, he cannot deny. The household of God has claims upon our tenderness in such matters which criticism and history have not.

§ 7.

For myself, I have no call or wish at all to write in behalf

missibility justifies us in blurting it out to the world at large. Such an act may not be an offence against the faith, but still is an offence against charity. A personal view of a certain theological opinion may not be heretical, as not being contradictory to any point of faith, yet in a particular time or place it may be so contrary to the dominant opinion in the Catholic body, as in Galileo's case, that zeal for the honour of the Divine Word, deference to existing authorities, charity towards the weak and ignorant, and distrust of self, should keep a man from being impetuous in circulating what nevertheless he considers to be true, that is, unless for one reason or other, freedom of speech is a duty in the particular case. To act otherwise would not be clear of sin. The household of God has claims upon our tenderness in such matters, which criticism and history have not.'

[1] B, 'and a received opinion open to doubt'. (Otherwise § 6 is as text.)

of such persons as think it a love of truth to have no 'love of the brethren'. I am indeed desirous of investigating for its own sake the limit of free thought consistently with the claims upon us of Holy Scripture; still, my especial interest in the inquiry is from my desire to assist those religious sons of the Church who are engaged in Biblical criticism and its attendant studies, and have a conscientious fear of transgressing the rule of faith; men who wish to ascertain how far their religion puts them under obligations and restrictions in their reasonings and inferences on such sub-jects,—what conclusions may, and what may not, be held without interfering with that internal assent which, if[1] they would be Catholics, they are bound to give to the written Word of God.[1] I[2] do but contemplate the inward peace of religious Catholics in their own persons.[2] Of course those who begin without belief in the religious aspect of the universe, are not likely to be brought to such belief by studying it merely on its secular side.

§ 8.

Here,[3] then, the main question before us being what it is that[4] a Catholic is free to hold about Scripture in general, or about its separate portions, or its statements, without compromising his firm inward assent to the dogmas of the Church, that is, to the *de fide* enunciations of Popes[5] and Councils, we have first of all to inquire how many, and what, those dogmas are.

I answer that there are two such dogmas; one relates to the authority of Scripture, the other to its interpretation.

[1-1] AB, 'which they are bound to give, if they would be Catholics, to the written Word of God'.

[2-2] Not in A.

[3] 'Here': AB, 'Now'.

[4] 'That' not in A.

[5] AB, 'Pope'.

As to the authority of Scripture, we hold it to be, in all matters of faith and morals, divinely inspired throughout; as to its interpretation, we hold that the Church is, in faith and morals, the one infallible expounder of that inspired text.

I begin with the question of its inspiration.

§ 9.

The books which constitute the canon of Scripture, or the Canonical books, are enumerated by the Tridentine Council, as we find them in the first page of our Catholic Bibles; and are in that Ecumenical Council's decree spoken of by implication as the work of inspired men. The Vatican Council speaks more distinctly, saying that the entire books, with all their parts, are divinely inspired, and adding an anathema upon impugners of this its definition.

There is another dogmatic phrase used by the Councils of Florence and Trent to denote the inspiration of Scripture, viz., 'Deus *unus et idem* utriusque Testamenti Auctor'. Since this left room for holding that by the word 'Testamentum' was meant 'Dispensation', as it seems to have meant in former Councils from the date of Irenæus, and as St Paul uses the word in his Epistle to the Hebrews, the Vatican Council has expressly defined that the concrete *libri* themselves of the Old and New Testament 'Deum habent Auctorem'.

§ 10.

There is a further question, which is still left in some ambiguity, the meaning of the word 'Auctor'. 'Auctor' is not identical with the English word 'Author'. Allowing that there are instances to be found in classical[1] Latin in

---

[1] A, 'classic'.

which 'auctores' may be translated 'authors', instances in
which it even seems to mean 'writers', it more naturally[1]
means 'authorities'. Its proper sense is 'originator', 'in-
ventor', 'founder', 'primary cause'; (thus St Paul speaks of
our Lord as 'Auctor salutis', 'Auctor fidei';) on the other
hand, that it was the inspired penmen who were the
'writers' of their respective[2] works seems asserted by St
John and St Luke, and, I may say, in every paragraph of
St Paul's Epistles. In St John we read, 'This is the disciple
who testifies of these things, and has *written* these things,'
and St Luke says, 'I have thought it good to *write* to thee,'
etc. However, if any one prefers to construe 'auctor' as
'author', or writer, let it be so—only, then there will be
two writers of the Scriptures, the divine and the
human.

§ 11.

And now comes the important question, in what respect
are the Canonical books inspired? It cannot be in every
respect, unless we are bound *de fide* to believe that 'terra in
æternum stat', and that heaven is above us, and that there
are no antipodes. And it seems unworthy of Divine Great-
ness, that the Almighty should, in His revelation of Himself to us, undertake mere secular duties, and assume the
office of a narrator, as such, or an historian, or geographer,
except so far as the secular matters bear directly upon the
revealed truth. The Councils of Trent and the Vatican
fulfil this anticipation; they tell us distinctly the object
and the promise of Scripture inspiration. They specify
'faith and moral conduct' as the drift of that teaching
which has the guarantee of inspiration. What we need, and
what is given us, is not how to educate ourselves for this

[1] A, 'exactly'.
[2] 'Respective': not in A or B.

life; we have abundant natural gifts for human society, and for the advantages which it secures; but our great want is how to demean ourselves in thought and deed towards our Maker, and how to gain reliable information on this urgent necessity.

§ 12.

Accordingly, four times does the Tridentine Council insist upon 'faith and morality' as the scope of inspired teaching. It declares that the 'Gospel' is 'the Fount of all *saving truth* and all *instruction in morals'*, that in the written books and in the unwritten traditions, the Holy Spirit dictating, this *truth* and *instruction* are contained. Then it speaks of the books and traditions, 'relating whether to *faith* or to *morals'*, and afterwards of 'the confirmation of *dogmas* and establishment of *morals'*. Lastly, it warns the Christian people, 'in matters of *faith* and *morals'*, against distorting Scripture into a sense of their own.

In like manner the Vatican Council pronounces that Supernatural Revelation consists *'in rebus divinis'*, and is *contained* 'in libris scriptis et sine scripto traditionibus'; and it also speaks of 'petulantia ingenia' advancing wrong interpretations of Scripture 'in rebus *fidei* et *morum* ad ædificationem *doctrinæ* Christianæ pertinentium.'

§ 13.

But while the Councils, as has been shown, lay down so emphatically the inspiration of Scripture in respect to 'faith and morals', it is remarkable that they do not say a word directly as to its inspiration in matters of fact. Yet

are we therefore to conclude that the record of facts in
Scripture does not come under the guarantee of its inspiration? we are not so to conclude, and for this plain reason : —
the sacred narrative, carried on through so many ages,
what is it but the very matter of our faith, and rule of our
obedience? what but that narrative itself is the supernatural teaching, in order to which inspiration is given?
What is the whole history, as it is[1] traced out in Scripture
from Genesis to Esdras, and thence on to the end of the
Acts of the Apostles, what is it but a manifestation of
Divine Providence, on the one hand interpretative (on a
large scale and with analogical applications) of universal
history, and on the other preparatory (typical and predictive) of the Evangelical Dispensation? Its pages breathe
of providence and grace, of our Lord, and of His work
and teaching, from beginning to end. It views facts in those
relations in which neither ancients, such as the Greek
and Latin classical historians, nor moderns, such as Niebuhr, Grote, Ewald, or Michelet, can view them. In this
point of view it has God for its author, even though the
finger of God traced no words but the Decalogue. Such is
the claim of Bible history in its substantial fulness to be
accepted *de fide* as true. In this point of view, Scripture
is inspired, not only in faith and morals, but in all
its parts which bear on faith, including matters of
fact.[2]

§ 14.

But what has been said leads to another serious question.
It is easy to imagine a Code of Laws inspired, or a formal

---

[1] 'As it is': not in A or B.
[2] 'Including matters of fact': A, 'or, as theologians say, in respect to
"*res et sententias*".'

prophecy, or a Hymn, or a Creed, or a collection[1] of Pro-
verbs. Such works may be short, precise, and homogeneous;
but inspiration on the one hand, and on the other a document, multiform and copious in its contents, as the Bible
is, are at first sight incompatible ideas, and destructive of
each other. How are we practically to combine the indubitable fact of a divine superintendence with the indubitable
fact of a collection of such various writings?

§ 15.

Surely then, if the revelations and lessons in Scripture
are addressed to us personally and practically, the presence
among us of a formal judge and standing expositor of its
words, is imperative. It is antecedently unreasonable to
'speech was, not in the persuasive words of human wisdom,
so obscure, the outcome of so many minds, times, and
places, should be given us from above without the safe-
guard of some authority; as if it could possibly, from the
nature of the case, interpret itself. Its inspiration does but
guarantee its truth, not its interpretation. How are private
readers satisfactorily to distinguish what is didactic and
what is historical, what is fact and what is vision, what is
allegorical and what is literal, what is idiomatic and what
is grammatical, what is enunciated formally and what
occurs *obiter*, what is only of temporary and what is of
lasting obligation? Such is our natural anticipation, and
it is only too exactly justified in the events of the last three
centuries, in the many countries where private judgment
on the text of Scripture has prevailed. The gift of inspiration requires as its complement the gift of infallibility.

Where then is this gift lodged, which is so necessary for

[1] 'Collection': A, 'set'.

the due use of the written word of God? Thus we are
introduced to the second dogma in respect to Holy Scripture taught by the Catholic Religion. The first is that Scripture is inspired, the second, that the Church is the infallible
interpreter of that inspiration.

§ 16.

That the Church, and therefore the Pope, is that Interpreter is defined in the following words: —

First by the Council of Trent: 'Nemo suâ prudentiâ
innixus, in rebus fidei et morum ad ædificationem doctrinæ Christianæ pertinentium, Sacram Scripturam ad suos
sensus contorquens, contra eum sensum quem tenuit et
tenet Sancta Mater Ecclesia, cujus est judicare de vero
sensu et interpretatione Scripturarum Sanctarum, aut
etiam contra unanimem consensum Patrum, ipsam Scripturam Sacram interpretari audeat.'[1]

Secondly by the Council of the Vatican: 'Nos, idem
Decretum [Tridentinum] renovantes, hanc illius mentem
esse declaramus, ut in rebus fidei et morum ad ædificationem doctrinæ Christianæ pertinentium, is pro vero sensu
Sacræ Scripturæ habendus sit, quem tenuit et tenet Sancta
Mater Ecclesia, cujus est judicare de vero sensu et interpretatione Scripturarum Sanctarum,' etc.[2]

---

[1] Denz. 786 [1507]. 'In matters of faith and morals which build up
Christian doctrine, let no one, relying on his own judgment and twist-
ing Holy Scripture to his own meaning, presume to interpret Scripture
against that sense which Holy Mother Church has held and holds
(since it belongs to her to judge concerning the true sense and interpretation of Holy Scripture,) nor against a unanimous consensus of the
Fathers.' (Tr. by R.M.)

[2] Denz. 1788 [3007]. 'We, renewing the same decree [of Trent], declare
its intention to have been that in matters of faith and morals which
go to build up Christian doctrine, that is to be held the true sense of
Holy Scripture which Holy Mother Church has held and holds, since it
belongs to her to judge concerning the true sense and interpretation of
Holy Scripture' etc. (Tr. by R.M.)

§ 17.

Since, then, there is in the Church an authority, divinely appointed and plenary, for judgment and for appeal in questions of Scripture interpretation, in matters of faith and morals, therefore, by the very force of the words, there is one such authority, and only one.

Again, it follows hence, that, when the legitimate authority has spoken, to resist its interpretation is a sin against the faith, and an act of heresy.

And from this again it follows, that, till the Infallible Authority formally interprets a passage of Scripture, there is nothing heretical in advocating a contrary interpretation, provided of course there is nothing in the act intrinsically inconsistent with the faith, or the *pietas fidei*, nothing of contempt or rebellion, nothing temerarious, nothing offensive or scandalous, in the manner of acting or the circumstances of the case. I repeat, I am all along inquiring what Scripture, by reason of its literal text,[1] obliges us to believe. An original view about Scripture or its parts may be as little contrary to the mind of the Church about it, as it need be an offence against its inspiration.

The proviso, however, or condition, which I have just made, must carefully be kept in mind. Doubtless, a certain interpretation of a doctrinal text may be so strongly supported by the Fathers, so continuous and universal, and so cognate and connatural with the Church's teaching, that it is virtually or practically as dogmatic as if it were a formal judgment delivered on appeal by the Holy See, and cannot be disputed except as the Church or Holy See opens its wording or its conditions.[2] Hence the Vatican Council says, 'Fide divinâ et Catholicâ ea omnia credenda sunt,

---

[1] 'Literal text': A, 'inspiration'.
[2] 'Its wording or its conditions': A, 'the way or the conditions for it'.

quæ in verbo Dei scripto vel tradito continentur, vel ab
Ecclesiâ sive solemni judicio, sive *ordinario* et *universali
magisterio*, tanquam divinitus revelata, credenda propo-
nuntur.'[1] And I repeat, that, though the Fathers were not
inspired, yet their united testimony is of supreme authority;[2] at the same time, since no Canon or List has been
determined of the Fathers, the practical rule of duty is
obedience to the voice of the Church.

§ 18.

Such then is the answer which I make to the main question which has led to my writing. I asked what obligation
of duty lay upon the Catholic scholar or man of science as
regards his critical treatment of the text and the matter
of Holy Scripture. And now I say that it is his duty, first,
never to forget that what he is handling is the Word of
God, which, by reason of the difficulty of always drawing
the line between what is human and what is divine, cannot be put on the level of other books, as it is now the
fashion to do, but has the nature[3] of a Sacrament, which
is outward and inward,[4] and a channel of supernatural
grace; and secondly, that, in what he writes upon it, or its
separate books, he is bound to submit himself internally,
and to profess to submit himself, in all that relates to faith
and morals, to the definite teaching[5] of Holy Church.

[1] Denz. 1792 [3011]. 'By divine and Catholic faith must be believed all
those things which are contained in the Word of God, whether as
written or as handed down, and are proposed by the Church, whether by
a solemn judgment or by the ordinary and universal magisterium, as
things revealed by God and commanding belief.' (Tr. by R.M.)
[2] A, 'yet it is forbidden "contra unanimem consensum patrum ipsam
Scripturam Sacram interpretari";'.
[3] Nature: A, 'sacredness'.
[4] 'Outward and inward': A, 'visible and invisible'.
[5] 'Definite teaching': A, 'judgment'.

This being laid down, let me go on to consider some of the critical distinctions and conclusions which are consistent with a faithful observance of these obligations.

§ 19.

Are the books or are the writers inspired? I answer, Both. The Council of Trent says the writers, 'ab ipsis Apostolis, Spiritu Sancto dictante';* the Vatican says the books, 'si quis libros integros etc. divinitus inspiratos esse negaverit, anathema sit.' Of course the Vatican decision is *de fide*, but it cannot annul the Tridentine. Both decrees are dogmatic truths. The Tridentine teaches us that the Divine Inspirer, inasmuch as He acted on the writer, acted, not immediately on the books themselves, but through the men who wrote them. The books are inspired, because the writers were inspired to write them. They are not inspired books, unless they came from inspired men.

There is one instance in Scripture of Divine Inspiration without a human medium: the Decalogue was written by the very finger of God. He wrote the Law upon the stone tables Himself. It has been thought that the Urim and Thummim was another instance of the immediate inspiration of a material substance; but anyhow such instances are exceptional; certainly, as regards Scripture, which alone concerns us here, there always have been two minds in the process of inspiration, a divine *Auctor*, and a human *Scriptor*; and various important consequences follow from this appointment.

* I omit what is said about Tradition, as not coming into my subject.[1]

[1] Note in A (headed 'NOTE.—') but not in B.

§ 20.

If there be at once a divine and a human mind co-operating in the formation of the sacred text, it is not surprising if there often be a double sense in that text, and (with obvious exceptions)[1] never certain that there is not.

Thus Sara had her human and literal meaning in her words, 'Cast out the bondwoman and her son', etc.; but we know from St Paul that those words were inspired by the Holy Ghost to convey a spiritual meaning. Abraham, too, on the Mount, when his son asked him whence was to come the victim for the sacrifice which his father was about to offer, answered 'God will provide'; and he showed his own sense of his words afterwards, when he took the ram which was caught in the briars, and offered it as a holocaust. Yet those words were a solemn prophecy.

And is it extravagant to say, that, even in the case of men who have no pretension to be prophets or servants of God, He may by their means give us great maxims and lessons, which the speakers little thought they were delivering? as in the case of the Architriclinus in the marriage feast, who spoke of the bridegroom as having 'kept the good wine until now'; words which it was needless for St John to record, unless they had a mystical meaning.

Such instances raise the question whether the Scripture saints and prophets always understood the higher and divine sense of their words. As to Abraham, this will be answered in the affirmative; but I do not see reason for thinking that Sara was equally favoured. Nor is her case solitary; Caiphas, as high priest, spoke a divine truth by virtue of his office, little thinking of it, when he said that 'one man must die for the people'; and St Peter at Joppa

---

[1] '(With obvious exceptions)': not in A.

at first did not see beyond a literal sense in his vision, though he knew that there was a higher sense, which in God's good time would be revealed to him.

And hence there is no difficulty in supposing that the Prophet Osee, though inspired, knew only[1] his own literal sense of the words which he transmitted to posterity, 'I have called my Son out of Egypt', the further prophetic meaning of them being declared by St Matthew in his gospel. And such a divine sense would be both concurrent with, and confirmed by, that antecedent belief which prevailed among the Jews in St. Matthew's time, that their sacred books were in great measure typical, with an evangelical bearing, though as yet they might not know what those books contained in prospect.

§ 21.

Nor is it *de fide* (for that alone with a view to Catholic Biblicists I am considering) that inspired men, at the time when they speak from inspiration, should always know that the Divine Spirit is visiting them.

The Psalms are inspired; but, when David, in the outpouring of his deep contrition, disburdened himself before his God in the words of the *Miserere* could he, possibly, while uttering them, have been directly conscious that every word he uttered was not simply his, but another's? Did he not think that he was personally asking forgiveness and spiritual help? Doubt again seems incompatible with a consciousness of being inspired. But Father Patrizi, while reconciling two Evangelists in a passage of their narratives, says, if I understand him rightly (ii, p. 405), that though we admit that there were some things about which

---

[1] 'Knew only': AB, 'only knew'.

inspired writers doubted, this does not imply that inspiration allowed them to state what is doubtful as certain, but
only it did not hinder them from stating things with a
doubt on their minds about them; but how can the All-
knowing Spirit doubt? or how can an inspired man doubt,
if he is conscious of his inspiration?

And again, how can a man whose hand is guided by
the Holy Spirit, and who knows it, make apologies for his
style of writing, as if deficient in literary exactness and
finish? If then the writer of Ecclesiasticus, at the very
time that he wrote his Prologue, was not only inspired, but
conscious of his inspiration, how could he have entreated
his readers to 'come with benevolence', and to make ex-
cuse for his 'coming short in the composition of words'?
Surely, if at the very time he wrote he had known it, he
would, like other inspired men, have said, 'Thus saith the
Lord,' or what was equivalent to it.

The same remark applies to the writer of the second book
of Machabees, who ends his narrative by saying, 'If I have
done well, it is what I desired, but if not so perfectly, it must
be pardoned me.' What a contrast to St Paul, who, speaking of his inspiration (1 Cor. vii, 40) and of his 'weakness
and fear' (*ibid.* ii, 4), does so in order to *boast* that his
'speech was, not in the persuasive words of human wisdom,
but in the showing of the Spirit and of power'. The historian of the Machabees would have surely adopted a like
tone of 'glorying', had he had at the time a like consciousness of his divine gift.

§ 22.

Again, it follows from there being two agencies, divine
grace and human intelligence, co-operating in the pro-

duction of the Scriptures, that, whereas, if they were written, as in the Decalogue, by the immediate finger of God, every word of them must be His and His only; on the contrary, if they are man's writing, informed and quickened[1] by the presence of the Holy Ghost, they admit, should it so happen, of being composed of outlying materials, which have passed through the minds and from the fingers of inspired penmen, and are known to be inspired on the ground that those who were the immediate editors, as they may be called, were inspired.

For an example of this we are supplied by the writer of the second book of Machabees, to which reference has already been made. 'All such things,' says the writer, 'as have been comprised in five books by Jason of Cyrene, we have attempted to abridge in one book.' Here we have the human aspect of an inspired work. Jason need not, the writer of the second book of Machabees must, have been inspired.

Again; St Luke's Gospel is inspired, as having gone through and come forth from an inspired mind; but the extrinsic sources of his narrative were not necessarily all inspired, any more than was Jason of Cyrene; yet such sources there were, for, in contrast with the testimony of the actual eye-witnesses of the events which he records, he says of himself that he wrote after a careful inquiry, 'according as *they* delivered them to us, who from the beginning were eye-witnesses and ministers of the word'; as to himself, he had but 'diligently attained to all things from the beginning'. Here it was not the original statements, but his edition of them, which needed to be inspired.

[1] 'Quickened': A, 'spiritualized'.

§ 23.

Hence we have no reason to be surprised, nor is it against the faith to hold, that a canonical book may be composed, not only from, but even of, pre-existing documents, it being always borne in mind, as a necessary condition, that an inspired mind has exercised a supreme and an ultimate judgment on the work, determining what was to be selected and embodied in it, in order to its truth in all 'matters of faith and morals pertaining to the edification of Christian doctrine', and its unadulterated truth.

Thus Moses may have incorporated in his manuscript as much from foreign documents as is commonly maintained by the critical school; yet the existing Pentateuch, with the miracles which it contains, may still (from that personal inspiration which belongs to a prophet) have flowed from his mind and hand on to his composition. He new-made and authenticated what till then was no matter of faith.

This[1] being considered, it follows that a book may be, and may be accepted as, inspired, though not a word of it

---

[1] In A this passage reads: 'This being considered, it follows that a book may be accepted and held as inspired, though not a word of it is an original document. Such is the case of St Matthew's Gospel. The Fathers agree that St Matthew wrote in Hebrew, and the Hebrew is lost. We have it in Greek, and the Greek is inspired. But why? Not merely because it is the translation of an inspired work; for a translation of such is not necessarily inspired itself, or else the Vulgate would be inspired. The reason why the translated Gospel of St Matthew is inspired must be, because not only St Matthew himself but his translator also was inspired, viz., in order to translate infallibly. Even if the Evangelist saw and approved the translation, this would not be enough to make it canonical, as the Vatican Council distinctly pronounces.*
The Book of Ecclesiasticus is another instance; it is a simple translation, and is inspired, not because the original compiler, but because his grandson, the translator, was inspired.'
'NOTE.—* "Qui quidem V. et N. Testamenti Libri . . . pro sacris et

is an original document. Such is almost the case with the
first book of Esdras. A learned writer in a publication of
the day* says: 'It consists of the contemporary historical
journals, kept from time to time by the prophets or other
authorised persons, who were eye-witnesses for the most
part of what they record, and whose several narratives were
afterwards strung together, and either abridged or added
to, as the case required, by a later hand, of course an
inspired hand.'[1]

And in like manner the Chaldee and Greek portions[2]
of the book of Daniel, even though not written by Daniel,
may be, and we believe are,[3] written by penmen inspired
in matters of faith and morals;[3] and so much, and nothing
beyond, does the Church 'oblige' us to believe.

§ 24.

I have said that the Chaldee, as well as the Hebrew portion of Daniel, requires, in order to its inspiration, not that
it should be Daniel's writing, but that its writer, whoever
he was, should be inspired. This leads me to the question
whether inspiration requires and implies that the book
inspired should, in its form and matter, be homogeneous,
and all its parts belong to each other. Certainly not. The
Book of Psalms is the obvious instance destructive of any

---

* Smith's *Dictionary of the Bible.*[4]

canonicis suscipiendi sunt . . . *non* ideo, quod solâ *humanâ* industriâ
concinnati, sua [Ecclesiae] *deinde* auctoritate sint approbati, nec ideo
dumtaxat, quod revelationem sine errore contineant, sed propterea, quod,
Spiritu Sancto inspirante conscripti Deum habent auctorem" etc.' (Denz.
1787 [3006]; for translation, see Introduction, p. 53).

[1] (End of divergence from A).
[2] 'And Greek portions': A, 'portion'.
[3-3] 'Are . . . morals': A, 'is, written by an inspired penman.'
[4] Note not in A: B, 'Smith's *Dictionary*'.

such idea. What it really requires is an inspired Editor;*
that is, an inspired mind, authoritative in faith and morals,
from whose fingers the sacred text passed. I believe it is
allowed generally that, at the date of the captivity and
under the persecution of Antiochus, the books of Scripture and the sacred text suffered much loss and injury.
Originally the Psalms seem to have consisted of five books,
of which only a portion, perhaps the first and second, were
David's. That arrangement is now broken up, and the
Council of Trent was so impressed with the difficulty of
their authorship, that, in its formal decree respecting the
Canon, instead of calling the collection 'David's Psalms,'
as was usual, they called it the 'Psalterium Davidicum,'
thereby meaning to imply, that, although canonical and
inspired and in spiritual fellowship and relationship with
those of 'the choice Psalmist of Israel,' the whole collection is not therefore[1] necessarily the writing of David.

And as the name of David, though not really applicable
to every Psalm, nevertheless protected and sanctioned
them all, so the appendices which conclude the book of
Daniel, Susanna and Bel, though not belonging to the
main history, come under the shadow of that Divine Presence, which primarily rests on what goes before.

And so again, whether or not the last verses of St Mark's,

* This representation must not be confused with either of the two
views of canonicity which are pronounced insufficient by the Vatican
Council, viz., 1, that in order to be sacred and canonical, it is enough
for a book to be a work of mere human industry, provided it be afterwards approved by the authority of the Church; and 2, that it is enough
if it contains revealed teaching without error. Neither of these views sup-
poses the presence of inspiration, whether in the writer or the writing;
what is contemplated above is an inspired writer in the exercise of his
inspiration, and a work inspired from first to last under the action of
that inspiration.[2]

[1] 'The whole collection is not therefore': A, 'they were not therefore
all'.

[2] Note not in A.

and two portions of St John's Gospel, belong to those Evangelists respectively, matters not as regards their inspiration; for the Church has recognised them as portions of that sacred narrative which precedes or embraces them.

Nor does it matter, whether one or two Isaiahs wrote the book which bears that Prophet's name; the Church, without settling this point, pronounces it inspired in respect of faith and morals, both Isaiahs being inspired; and, if this be assured to us, all other questions are irrelevant and unnecessary.

Nor do the Councils forbid our holding that there are interpolations or additions in the sacred text, say, the last chapter of the Pentateuch, provided they are held to come from an inspired penman, such as Esdras, and are thereby authoritative in faith and morals.

§ 25.

From what has been last said it follows, that the titles of the Canonical books, and their ascription to definite authors, either do not come under their inspiration, or need not be accepted literally.

For instance: the Epistle to the Hebrews is said in our Bibles to be the writing of St Paul, and so virtually it is, and to deny that it is so in any sense might be temerarious; but its authorship is not a matter of faith as its inspiration is, but an acceptance of[1] received opinion, and because to no other writer can it be so well assigned.

Again, the 89th Psalm has for its title 'A Prayer of Moses', yet that has not hindered a succession of Catholic writers, from Athanasius to Bellarmine, from denying it to be his.

---

[1] 'Acceptance of': A, 'acquiescence in'.

E

Again, the Book of Wisdom professes (*e.g.*, chs. vii and ix) to be written by Solomon; yet our Bibles say, 'It is written in the *person* of Solomon,' and[1] 'it is uncertain who was the writer'; and St Augustine, whose authority had so much influence in the settlement of the Canon, speaking of Wisdom and Ecclesiasticus, says: 'The two books, by reason of a certain similarity of style,[2] are usually called Solomon's, though the more learned have no doubt they do not belong to him.' (Martin. *Pref. to Wisdom and Eccl.*; Aug. *Opp.* t. iii, p. 733.)

If these instances hold, they are precedents for saying that it is no sin against the faith (for of such I have all along been speaking), nor indeed, if done conscientiously and on reasonable grounds, any sin, to hold that Ecclesiastes is not the writing of Solomon, in spite of its opening with a profession of being his; and that first, because that profession is a heading, not a portion of the book; secondly, because, even though it be part of the book, a like profession is made in the Book of Wisdom, without its being a proof that 'Wisdom' is Solomon's; and thirdly, because such a profession may well be considered a prosopopœia not so difficult to understand as that of the Angel Raphael, when he called himself 'the Son of the great Ananias'.

On this subject Melchior Canus says: 'It does not much matter to the Catholic Faith that a book was written by this or that writer, so long as the Spirit of God is believed to be the Author of it; which Gregory delivers and explains in his Preface to Job, "It matters not," he says,[3] "with what pen the King has written His letter, if it be true that He has written it."' (*Loc. Th.* p. 44.)

I say then of the Book of Ecclesiastes, its authorship is

---

[1] 'And': A, 'but'.
[2] 'Style': A, 'doctrine'.
[3] 'He says': not in A or B.

one of those questions which still lie[1] in the hands of the
Church. If the Church formally declared that it was written
by Solomon, I consider that, in accordance with[2] its heading (and, as implied in what follows, as in 'Wisdom',) we
should be bound, recollecting that she has the gift of
judging 'de vero sensu et interpretatione Scripturarum
Sanctarum', to accept such a decree as a matter of faith;
and in like manner, in spite of its heading, we should be
bound to accept a contrary decree, if[3] made to the effect
that the book was not Solomon's. At present, as the Church
(or Pope) has not pronounced on one side or on the other,
I conceive that, till a decision comes from Rome, either
opinion is open to the Catholic without any impeachment
of his faith.

§ 26.

And here I am led on to inquire whether *obiter dicta*
are conceivable in an inspired document. We know that
they are held to exist, and even required, in treating of the
dogmatic utterances of Popes, but are they compatible with
inspiration? The common opinion is that they are not. Professor Lamy thus writes about them, in the form of an
objection: 'Many minute matters occur in the sacred
writers which have regard only to human feebleness and
the natural necessities of life, and by no means require
inspiration, since they can otherwise be perfectly well
known, and seem scarcely worthy of the Holy Spirit, as for
instance what is said of the dog of Tobias, St Paul's *penula*,
and the salutations at the end of the Epistles.' Neither he
nor Fr Patrizi allow of these exceptions; but Fr Patrizi,

[1] 'Still lie': A, 'is'.
[2] 'In accordance with': A, 'on account of'.
[3] 'If', not in A.

as Lamy quotes him, 'damnare non audet eos qui hæc tenerent', [viz., exceptions,][1] and he himself, by keeping silence, seems unable to condemn them either.

By *obiter dicta* in Scripture I also mean such statements as we find in the Book of Judith, that Nabuchodonosor was King of Nineve. Now it is in favour of there being such unauthoritative *obiter dicta*, that, unlike those which occur in dogmatic utterances of Popes and Councils, they are, in Scripture, not doctrinal, but mere unimportant statements of fact; whereas those of Popes and Councils may relate to faith and morals, and are said to be uttered *obiter*, because they are not contained within the scope of the formal definition, and imply no intention of binding the consciences of the faithful. There does not then seem any serious difficulty in admitting their existence in Scripture. Let it be observed, its miracles are doctrinal facts, and in no sense of the phrase can be considered *obiter dicta*.

§ 27.

It may be questioned, too, whether the absence of chronological sequence might not be represented as an infringement of plenary inspiration more serious than the *obiter dicta* of which I have been speaking. Yet St Matthew is admitted by approved commentators to be unsolicitous as to order of time. So says Fr Patrizi (*De Evang.* lib. ii, p. 1), viz., 'Matthæum de observando temporis ordine minime sollicitum esse'. He gives instances, and then repeats 'Matthew did not observe order of time'.[2] If such absence of order is compatible with inspiration in St Matthew, as it is, it might be consistent with inspiration in parts of the

[1] '[viz., exceptions,]': not in A.
[2] A added here: 'A later commentator thus arranges portions of his chapters: 8, 4, 5, 8 . . . 13, 8, 9, 13 . . . 14, 18, 20, 26, 21.'

Old Testament, supposing they are open to re-arrangement in chronology. Does not this teach us to fall back upon the decision of the Councils that 'faith and morals pertaining to the edification of Christian doctrine' are the scope, the true scope, of inspiration? And is not the Holy See the judge given us for determining what is for edification and what is not?

There is another practical exception to the ideal continuity of Scripture inspiration in mere matters of fact, and that is the multitude of various manuscript readings which surround the sacred text. Unless we have the text as inspired men wrote it, we have not the divine gift in its fulness, and as far as we have no certainty which out of many is the true reading, so far, wherever the sense is affected, we are in the same difficulty as may be the consequence of an *obiter dictum*. Yet, in spite of this danger, even cautious theologians do not hesitate to apply the gratuitous hypothesis of errors in transcription as a means of accounting for such statements of fact as they feel to need an explanation. Thus Fr Patrizi, not favouring the order of our Lord's three temptations in the desert, as given by St Luke, attributes it to the mistake of the transcribers. 'I have no doubt at all,' he says, 'that it is to be attributed, not to Luke himself, but to his transcribers' (*ibid*. p. 5); and again, he says that it is owing 'vitio librariorum' (p. 394). If I recollect rightly, Melchior Canus has recourse to the 'fault of transcribers' also. Indeed it is commonly urged in controversy (*vide* Lamy, i. p. 31).

§ 28.

I do not here go on to treat of the special instance urged against us by M. Renan, drawn from the Book of Judith, because I have wished to lay down principles, and next, because his charge can neither be proved nor refuted just now, while the strange discoveries are in progress about Assyrian and Persian history by means of the cuneiform inscriptions. When the need comes, the Church, or the Holy See, will interpret the sacred book for us.

I conclude by reminding the reader that in these remarks I have been concerned only with the question— what have Catholics to hold and profess *de fide* about Scripture? that is, what it is the Church 'insists' on their holding; and next, by unreservedly submitting what I have written to the judgment of the Holy See, being more desirous that the question should be satisfactorily answered, than that my own answer should prove to be in every respect the right one.

JOHN H. CARDINAL NEWMAN.[1]

---

[1] Not in A.

§ 29.

NOTE[1]

On the Phrase 'Auctor utriusque Testamenti' in the Councils.

Does it mean Inspirer of the Scriptures, or Author of the two Dispensations or Covenants—viz., of the Old as well as of the New?

I consider it has the latter meaning, being directed against the heresy, so early and so late, of Gnostics, Manichees, Priscillianists, and Paulicians, that the God of the Old Testament was not the God of the New. On the contrary, in a succession of protests, the Church from the beginning asserts that there is but one God of both Dispensations; that one and the same God is the Author of the one and the other. He who originated the New Covenant also originated the Old. The heresy anathematised was not that the Scriptures were not inspired, but that the God of the New Dispensation was not the God of the Old.

1. St Irenæus, A.D. 200, is one of the earliest writers who protests against this heretical doctrine, and he throws light upon a subsequent series of Councils down to the Tridentine. He never confuses between 'Testaments' and 'Scriptures'; with him, Testament means Covenant or Dispensation. Sometimes he speaks of the Old Testament as 'The Law', as our Lord speaks of 'The Law and the Prophets', not Prophetic writings. The New Testament he calls the Gospel—viz., in the abstract. In one place he

[1] This Note is in A but not in B.

speaks of *four* Testaments, those of Adam, Noe, Moses, and Christ. *Contra Hæreses*, Liber iii, c. xi, § 8.[1] Speaking of the two, he says, 'Non alterum [Auctorem] Vetera, alterum proferentem Nova docuit, sed *unum et eundem*'. Liber iv, c. ix, § 1.[2] Again, '*Utraque* Testamenta *unus et idem* Paterfamilias produxit.' *Ibid.*[3]

2. So the Spanish and Portuguese Council of A.D. 447 against the Priscillianists, 'Si quis dixerit *alterum* Deum esse priscæ Legis, *alterum* Evangeliorum, anathema sit'.

3. Again, 'Credo Novi et Veteris Testamenti, Legis, et Prophetarum et Apostolorum, *unum* esse Auctorem, Deum Omnipotentem', etc. S. Leo IX, A.D. 1050.

4. The profession of the Waldenses on their submission, 'Novi et Veteris Testamenti *unum eundem* Auctorem esse Dominum credimus'. A.D. 1210.

5. 'Credimus Novi et Veteris Testamenti, Legis ac Prophetarum et Apostolorum, *unum* esse Auctorem Deum.' *Conf. M. Palæolog.*, A.D. 1274.

6. Pope Eugenius IV, A.D. 1439. '*Unum atque eundem* Deum Veteris et Novi Testamenti, hoc est, Legis et Prophetarum, atque Evangelii, profitetur Auctorem, quoniam, eodem Spiritu Sancto inspirante, *utriusque* Testamenti *Sancti* locuti sunt, quorum *libros* suscipit et veneratur.'

7. Council of Trent. It only goes as far as Irenæus.[4] 'Omnes *libros* tam Veteris quam Novi Testamenti, cum *utriusque* [not omnium] *unus* Deus sit auctor, . . . *suscipit* et veneratur.'

8.[5] It is true that the Vatican Council has made the

---

[1] Reference not in A.
[2] Reference not in A.
[3] Not in A.
[4] 'It . . . Irenaeus': not in A.
[5] A has only: '8. The above is only noted historically, for the Vatican Council has defined Auctor Testamenti to be Auctor Scripturarum.' (No footnote.)

words 'Auctor Scripturarum' equivalent to 'Inspiration', but when it so spoke it was engaged upon the subject of 'morals and religion', not upon profane history, etc. *Vide* Abp. Mac Evilly; 2 Timothy, c. iii, v. 16, 17.*

* 'In the Greek, the word "is" is understood, so as to convey two assertions: first, all Scripture is inspired of God; and secondly, Scripture thus inspired is also useful for the purposes of instruction, etc. According to our Vulgate reading there is only one assertion conveyed, viz., that all Scripture that is inspired of God is profitable for instructing the ignorant in the truths of faith, for refuting the errors opposed to sound doctrine, for rebuking men of corrupt principles and morals, and for forming men to sanctity and Christian justice. These are the four great duties of a minister of religion, and for these the S. Scripture is profitable. It is quite evident that this passage furnishes no argument whatever that the S. Scripture, without Tradition, is the *sole rule of faith*; for, although S. Scripture is *profitable* for these four ends, still it is not said to be *sufficient*. The Apostle requires the aid of Tradition (2 Thessalonians, ii, 15). Moreover, the Apostle here refers to the Scriptures which Timothy was taught in his infancy. Now, a good part of the New Testament was not written in his boyhood: some of the Catholic Epistles were not written even when St Paul wrote this, and none of the Books of the New Testament were then placed on the canon of Scripture books. He refers, then, to the Scriptures of the *Old* Testament, and if the argument from this passage proved anything, it would prove too much, viz., that the Scriptures of the *New* Testament were not necessary for a rule of faith.

It is hardly necessary to remark that this passage furnishes no proof of the inspiration of the several books of S. Scripture, even of those admitted to be such. According to the Vulgate reading of this verse (16), which Bloomfield assures us is adopted by all the most eminent critics after Theodoret, there is nothing said of the inspiration of any part of Scripture; all that is stated is simply this: that every portion of inspired Scripture is profitable for teaching, reproving, etc., without determining what these inspired Scriptures are. Nor is the question determined by the Greek reading either. For we are not told what is meant by "every Scripture" of which it is said, according to this reading, that it "is inspired", or what the Books or portions of "inspired Scripture" are.'

E*

ESSAY II

FURTHER ILLUSTRATIONS

§ 30.

Prefatory Notice[1]

In the February Number of the *Nineteenth Century*, an article of mine appeared, which has elicited a criticism from a Catholic Professor of name. As I acquiesce neither in his statements nor in his reasonings, I have been[2] led to put on paper Remarks[3] in answer to him; and that without availing myself of the offer made to me by the Editor of the Review to re-publish, together with these Remarks,[4] my Article itself: an indulgence beyond its rules, which I feel I have no right to accept, unless the Article shall be expressly called for by the public.

At present, in order to make these Remarks[5] intelligible to those who have not seen my original Article, it is sufficient, I conceive, to say that they aim, as that Article did, at answering the question proposed in my title-page:* 'What is of obligation for a Catholic to believe concerning the Inspiration of the Canonical Scriptures?' This being the sole question, I observed, that, since two Ecumenical Councils have spoken upon Inspiration, it is obvious to

---

* The original title-page.[6]

---

[1] C has title as given in *Note on Presentation of the Text*: text begins with heading 'NOTICE'.

[2] 'Have been': C, 'am'.

[3] C, 'a Postscript'.

[4] C, 'this Postscript'.

[5] C, 'this Postscript'.

[6] Not in C.

have recourse to them, if we would learn what is *de fide*,
or obligatory on our faith in the matter. To this, of course,
must be added any teaching which comes to us incidentally from the ordinary *magisterium* of the Church, or from
the joint testimony of the Fathers; but the two Councils,
the Tridentine and the Vatican, give us by far the most
distinct and definite information.

These two Councils decide that the Scriptures are inspired, and inspired throughout, but[1] they do not add to
their decision that they are inspired by an immediately
divine act, but they say that they are inspired[1] through
the instrumentality of inspired men; that they are inspired
in all matters of faith and morals, meaning thereby, not
only theological doctrine, but also the historical and pro-
phetical narratives which they contain, from Genesis to
the Acts of the Apostles; and lastly, that, being inspired
because written by inspired men, they have a human side,
which manifests itself in language, style, tone of thought,
character, intellectual peculiarities, and such infirmities,
not sinful, as belong to our nature, and which in unimportant matters may issue in what in doctrinal definitions is
called an *obiter dictum*. At the same time, the gift of
inspiration being divine, a Catholic must never forget that
what he is handling is in a true sense the Word of God,
which, as I said in my Article, 'by reason of the difficulty
of always drawing the line between what is human and
what is divine, cannot be put on the level of other books,
as it is now the fashion to do, but has the nature of a
Sacrament, which is outward and inward, and a channel
of supernatural grace'.

This is why the second great definition of the Councils,
on which I proceeded in my Article to insist, is so impor-

[1-1] C, 'but not inspired by an immediately divine act, but through. . . .'

tant, viz., that 'the authoritative interpretation of Scripture rests with the Church'.

So much on the view of Scripture which offends the Professor in question,[1] to whose criticisms in the March Number of[2] the *Irish Ecclesiastical Record* I now make my answer.

§ 31.

Prefatory Notice (continued)[3]

A not over-courteous, nor over-exact writer, in his criticisms on my Essay on Inspiration, gives it as his judgment upon it, that 'its startling character' must be evident to 'the merest tyro in the schools of Catholic Theology'. 'Tis a pity he did not take more than a short month for reading, pondering, writing, and printing. Had he not been in a hurry to publish, he would have made a better Article. I took above a twelve-month for mine. Thus I account for some of the Professor's unnecessary remarks.

If I understand him, his main *thesis* is this—that, virtually or actually, Scripture is inspired, not only in matters of faith and morals, as is declared in the Councils of Trent and of the Vatican, but in all respects, and for all purposes, and on all subjects; so that no clause all through the Bible is liable to criticism[4] of any kind, and that no good Catholic can think otherwise. If this is his position, it is plain that I approach the question on quite a distinct side from his; but I do not see that personally and practically I have very much to differ from him in, except in his faulty logic, and his misrepresentations of what I have written.

---

[1] 'The Professor in question': C, 'Professor Healy'.
[2] 'The March Number of': not in C.
[3] In C, heading is 'POSTSCRIPT'.
[4] 'Liable to criticism': C, 'open to the charge of error'.

§ 32.

Divine Inspiration of Scripture in all matters of Faith and Morals

This proposition must be accepted as *de fide*, or of obligatory faith, by every Catholic, as having been so defined by the Councils of Trent and of the Vatican.

Now I say first, that the inspiration of religious and moral truth, of which these Councils speak, is a divine gift, in the first instance given to divine ministers, and from them carried on, as into their oral teachings, so also into such of their writings as the Church has declared to be sacred and canonical.

And next: divine gifts, as we read of them in the history of Revelation, did not extend in every case to all departments of ministration, but had in each instance a particular service and application. These various favours were ordinarily but partial, given for precise and definite purposes; so that it is but in harmony with the rule of Providence in parallel cases, if there should be found, in respect to Biblical Inspiration, a distribution and a limitation in the bestowal of it. St Paul's account of the *gratiæ gratis datæ*, may be taken to illustrate this principle, without my meaning at all thereby to imply that the inspiration of an Evangelist was not in its intensity, refinement, abundance, and manifoldness, far superior to the gifts spoken of by the Apostle in the chapter to which I refer. I refer to that chapter in order to draw attention to what was the rule of Providence at the first in the disposal and direction of the *gratiæ gratis datæ*, viz., that they had a special scope and character, and, in consequence, as is intimated in the parable of the Five and Ten Talents, were limited in their range of operation. I am not here affirming or denying that Scripture is inspired in matters of astronomy and chronology, as well as in faith and morals; but I certainly do not see that because Inspiration is given for the latter subjects, therefore it extends to the former.

The Apostle tells us that, whereas there are '*diversities* of grace', there is 'the *same* Spirit'; and that 'the manifestation of the Spirit is given to every man *unto profit*'; that is, the gift is given according to the measure of the need. Then he says, 'To one by the Spirit is given the Word of Wisdom, to another the Word of Knowledge according to the same Spirit'. To both of them there was given 'the Word' of God; but one was the minister of the Word as far as Wisdom went, and the other as far as Knowledge went; and, though the same man might indeed have both gifts, we could not logically argue that he had wisdom on the mere ground of his having knowledge.

It may be observed too that it was by information from those who thus had 'the Word' of God that St Luke wrote his Gospel; for he says expressly that the things which he recorded 'were delivered to us' by those 'who from the beginning were eye-witnesses, and servants of the *Word*'; that is, those who saw, or who were inspired to know, what the Evangelist reported from them: a statement which would imply that their particular gift was that of bearing faithful witness, or otherwise being endowed with the gift of knowledge. As another instance of the limitation of a gift, I may refer to the history of Jonas. 'The Word of the Lord' came to him to denounce judgment against Nineve; but he did not know that the divine menace was conditional. Again, Eliseus says to Giezi, 'Was not my *heart present* when the man turned back to meet thee?' yet, when the Sunamitess had 'caught hold on his feet', he had said, 'Her soul is in anguish, and the Lord hath hid it from me and hath not told me.'

I return to St Paul: he continues, 'To another, Faith in

the same Spirit; to another, the grace of healing in one Spirit; to another, the working of miracles; to another, prophecy', and so on. He ends a long chapter on the subject by enumerating the offices which needed and determined the gifts—'Apostles, Prophets, Doctors', and the rest; and by intimating that, as not all are Apostles or Prophets, so the gifts, necessary to these, were not given to others. This is from 1 Cor. xii. The 4th Chapter of his epistle to the Ephesians is on the same subject.

I should infer from this, that those who were chosen by the Spirit to minister between God and man, such as Moses, Samuel, Elias, Isaias, the Apostles and Evangelists, would be invested with the high gifts necessary for their work, and not necessarily with other gifts.

I do not, then, feel it any difficulty when I am told by the infallible voice of more than one Ecumenical Council, that the writers of Scripture, whether under the New Covenant or the Old, ethical and religious writers as they were,[1] have had assigned to them a gift and promise in teaching which is in keeping with this antecedent idea which we form of the work of Evangelists and Prophets. If they are to teach us our duty to God and man, it is natural that inspiration should be promised them in matters of faith and morals; and if such is the actual promise, it is natural that Councils should insist upon its being such;—but how otherwise are we to account for the remarkable stress laid on the inspiration of Scripture in matters of faith and morals, both in the Vatican and at Trent, if after all faith and morals, in view of inspiration, are only parts of a larger gift? Why was it not simply said once for all that in all matters of faith or fact, not only in all its parts, but on every subject whatever, Scripture was inspired? If nothing short of the highest and exactest truth on all subjects must be contemplated

---

[1] 'As they were': not in C.

as the gift conveyed to the inspired writers, what is gained
by singling out faith and morals as the legitimate province
of Inspiration, and thereby throwing the wider and more
complete view of Scripture truth into the shade? Why, on
the contrary, does the Vatican Council so carefully repeat
the very wording of the Tridentine in its statements about
inspiration in faith and morals, putting no other subject
matter on a level with them? It may perhaps be said that
it is a rule with Councils, that the later repeat the very
words of the earlier; true, the Holy Trinity, the Creation,
the Incarnation, the Blessed Virgin's prerogatives, are often
expressed in language carrying on a tradition of terms as
well as truths; but this is done because the truths or words
are important. It is a paradox to say that the Vatican
declarations about Scripture are in their wording so much
of a *fac simile* of the Tridentine, only because they mean
so very little. Even when a phrase is not easy to translate,
the identity is preserved; for instance, the clause 'in rebus
fidei et morum, ad ædificationem doctrinæ Christianæ pertinentium', not 'pertinentibus', is found in both Councils.

This is the obvious aspect under which I first view the
inspiration of Scripture, as determined by the Councils.

§ 33.

Inspiration in matters of Historical Fact

Here we are brought to a second and most important
question. When I say that the writers of Scripture were
divinely inspired in all matters of faith and morals, what
matters are included in the range of such inspiration? Are
historical statements of fact included? It makes me smile
to think that any one could fancy me so absurd as to exclude them, especially since in a long passage in my Essay

I have expressly included them; but the Professor has done his best so to manage my text, as to make his readers believe that the Bible, as far as it is historical, does not in my view proceed from inspired writers. Professing to quote me, he omits just the very passage in which I have distinctly avowed the inspiration of the whole of its history. This is so strange, so anomalous a proceeding, as to make it difficult to believe that the same person who had the good feeling to write the first page of the Review wrote those which follow.

I am obliged to take notice of this great impropriety in pure self-defence; for if I am not able to show that the writer has ill-treated me, he will have an argument against me stronger than any which by fair means he is able to produce. On the other hand, if I show that he has been guilty of an indefensible act, third parties will not be so ready to think him a safe guide in other judgments which he makes to my discredit.

To begin, then: in § 13 of my Essay, pp. 5, 6, I write thus: 'While the Councils, as has been shown, lay down so emphatically the inspiration of Scripture in respect to faith and morals, it is remarkable that they do not say a word directly as to its inspiration in matters of fact. Yet are we therefore to conclude that the record of facts in Scripture does not come under the guarantee of its inspiration? *we are not so to conclude.*'

These are my words, as they stand; but he quotes them thus: '[The Cardinal] asserts that, while the Councils, as has been shown, lay down so emphatically the inspiration of Scripture in respect to faith and morals, it is remarkable that they do not say a word directly as to its inspiration in matters of fact', p. 139; *and there he stops:* he quotes neither my question nor my answer which follow my question being,

Qu.: 'Are we therefore to conclude that the record of facts in Scripture does not come under the guarantee of its inspiration?'
and my answer being,

Answ.: 'We are not so to conclude, and for this plain reason,' etc., etc.

With such notions of a critic's duty, much less does the Professor think it necessary to quote, or, I suppose, even to read, the twenty lines on behalf of the inspiration of the Bible history which follow thus:

'For this plain reason—the sacred narrative, carried on through so many ages, what is it but the very matter for our faith and rule of our obedience? What but that narrative itself is the supernatural teaching, in order to which inspiration is given? What is the whole history, traced out in Scripture from Genesis to Esdras, and thence on to the end of the Acts of the Apostles, but a manifestation of Divine Providence, on the one hand interpretative, on a large scale and with analogical applications, of universal history, and on the other preparatory, typical and predictive, of the Evangelical Dispensation? Its pages breathe of providence and grace, of our Lord, and of His work and teaching, from beginning to end. It views facts in those relations in which neither ancients, such as the Greek and Latin classical historians, nor moderns, such as Niebuhr, Grote, Ewald, or Michelet, can view them. In this point of view it has God for its Author, even though the finger of God traced no words but the Decalogue. Such is the claim of Bible history in its substantial fulness to be accepted *de fide* as true. *In this point of view, Scripture is inspired, not only in faith and morals, but in all its parts which bear on faith, including matters of fact.'*

All this he leaves out.

If a finish was wanting to this specimen of, what I must

call,[1] sharp practice, he has taken care to supply it. For, after cutting off my own statement at its third line, as I have shown, he substitutes, as if mine, a statement of his own, which he attributes to me, about *obiter dicta*, adding the words, '*Hence* he [the Cardinal] raises the question', which I do not raise till eight pages later, and not 'hence' even then. And next, whereas *obiter dicta* are according to him in their very nature exceptions to a rule, viz., the rule that Scripture statements of fact are inspired, he is obliged for the moment to imply that I do maintain the rule, in order that he may be able to impute to me, in cases of *obiter dicta*, a breach of it.

§ 34.

Obiter Dicta viewed relatively to Inspiration

The subject which naturally comes next to be considered is that of the possible presence of *obiter dicta* in inspired Scripture; by *obiter dicta* being meant phrases, clauses, or sentences in Scripture about matters of mere fact, which, as not relating to faith and morals, may without violence be referred to the human element in its composition.

Here, however, I observe with satisfaction that the Professor so far does me justice as to allow that what I have conceded, or have proposed to concede, to the scientific or literary inquirer, is not inconsistent with what the Church pronounces to be obligatory *de fide* on the Catholic. He says, 'while the Church is silent, we of course do not dare to censure these views, but neither do we dare to hold them'. This being the case, I shall, in the interest of the untheological student, under correction of the Church,

---

[1] 'What I must call': not in C.

continue as I have begun, to treat my subject as a question open to argument.

1. Now I observe, first, that any statement about the inspiration of Scripture is far too serious a matter in its bearings to be treated carelessly; and consequently the Professor explains, while he complains of, my 'raising the question' of *obiter dicta* 'and not answering it'. Of course; I do not go further in my Essay than saying, 'There does not seem any serious difficulty in admitting' that they are to be found in Scripture. Why is not that enough for a cautious man to say? The decision of the point does not rest with me; but still I may have an opinion as long as there is no decision.

2. And next, why does he always associate an *obiter dictum* with the notion of error or moral infirmity,[1] or, even as he sometimes expresses himself, with '*falsehood*'? At least what right has he to attribute such an association to me? I have implied no such thing. I very much doubt whether I have even once used the word 'error' in connection with the phrase 'obiter dictum', though (as I shall show directly) no harm follows if I have. I have given my own sense of the word when I parallel it to such instances of it as occur in a question of dogma. Does the Professor mean to say that such a *dictum* is necessarily false when it occurs in a dogmatic document? No—it is merely unauthoritative. Mind, I am not arguing that such an unauthoritative *dictum* is possible in a matter of inspired Scripture on the ground that it is possible in a matter of dogma; but I am showing by a parallel case what my own meaning of the word is.

Obiter dictum means, as I understand it, a phrase or sentence which, whether a statement of literal fact or not, is not from the circumstances binding on our faith. The

[1] 'Or moral infirmity': not in C.

force of the '*obiter*' is negative, not positive. To say, 'I do not accept a statement as a literal fact', is not all one with saying that it is *not* a fact; I can *not hold* without *holding not*. The very comfort of an *obiter dictum* to the Catholic, whether in its relation to infallibility or to inspiration, whether in dogma or in Scripture, is, that it enables him in controversy to pass by a difficulty, which else may be pressed on him without his having the learning perhaps, or the knowledge, or the talent, to answer it; that it enables him to profess neither Yes nor No in questions which are beyond him, and on which nothing depends. In difficult questions it leaves the Catholic student in peace. And, if my Critic[1] asks, as I understand him to do, who shall decide what is important and what is not, I answer at once, the Church, which, though he seems to forget it, claims the supreme interpretation of Scripture according to the force of that second dogma about the written Word which was defined both at Trent and the Vatican.

It is plain then, as an *obiter dictum*, in my understanding of it, does not oblige us to affirm or to deny the literal sense, neither does it prohibit us from passing over the literal sense altogether, and, if we prefer, from taking some second, third, or fourth interpretation of the many which are possible, (provided the Church does not forbid,) as I shall show from St Thomas presently.

3. And now take one of the instances with which Scripture may be said to provide us. St Paul speaks of 'the cloak which he left at Troas with Carpus'. Would St Timothy, to whom he wrote, think this an infallible utterance? And supposing it had been discovered, on most plausible evidence, that the Apostle left his cloak with Eutychus, not with Carpus, would Timothy, would Catholics now, make themselves unhappy, because St Paul had committed what

---

[1] C, 'the Professor'.

the Professor calls 'a falsehood'? Would Christians declare
that they had no longer any confidence in Paul after he
had so clearly shown that he 'had' *not* 'the Spirit of God'?
Would they feel that he had put the whole Apostolic
system into confusion, and by mistaking Eutychus for
Carpus he had deprived them henceforth of reading
with any comfort his Epistle to the Romans or to the
Ephesians?

I fear seeming to use light words on a sacred subject;
but I must ask, is St Paul's request to Timothy about his
penula, a portion of[1] 'the Word'? is it more than an apparent exception, in the text of his Epistle, to the continuity of the Divine Inspiration? And was not that continuity still without any break at all in St Paul, if we
consider Inspiration as a supernatural habit? May I ask an
urgent, important question without profaneness? Could St
Paul say, 'Thus saith the Lord, Send the penula', etc., etc.?
I do not deny, however, that in a certain case he could so
speak; but are we driven to that hypothesis here?

Theology has its prerogatives and rights; but its very
perfection as a science causes theologians to be somewhat
wanting in tenderness to concrete humanity, to those lay
Catholics who in their grasp of religious truth do not go
much beyond the catechism, and who, without entering
into the expedients which system demands, wish to preserve their obedience to Holy Church.

4. Let us see, however, whether St Thomas, the greatest
of theologians, will not accompany at least my first step
in this question.

In his Summa, i, qu. 102, he takes for granted the Inspiration of Scripture, and its truthfulness as the consequence of
that inspiration; for where truth is not an effect, inspiration is not a cause. And he inquires what statements of

---

[1] 'A portion of': not in C.

fact in Scripture are to be taken as true literally, and what
are not; and, in answer to the question, he lays down, as a
rule or test, decisive of the point, this circumstance, viz.,
whether the *manner* or *bearing* of the sacred writer is
historical or not. This being kept in mind, let us consider
his words:—

'In omnibus quæ *sic* [per modum narrationis historicæ]
Scriptura tradit, est pro fundamento tenenda veritas his-
toriæ'; that is, 'In all matters which Scripture delivers after
the manner of historical narrative, we must hold, as a
fundamental fact, the truth of the history.'

Now observe what follows from this. In giving a *rule* or
test of the *truth* of historical statements, he surely implies
that there are, or at least that there may be, statements
which do *not* embody, which do not profess to embody,
historical truth. If, in a military gathering or review, I were
told, 'You may know the English by their red coats', would
not this imply that there were troops on the ground who
were *not* English and *not* in red? And in like manner,
when St Thomas says that the test of historical truth is
the inspired penman's writing in the historical style, he
certainly implies that there are, or might be, statements of
fact, which in their literal sense come short of the historic
style and of historic truth, or are what I should call *obiter
dicta.* I repeat, *obiter dicta* are but 'unhistoric statements'.
So far I consider I speak with the sanction of St Thomas;
now let me go on to say what I hold without (as I fear) his
sanction.

5. I feel very diffident of my ability to speak with ever
so much restraint of the words of St Thomas; but, if I am
forced to speak, certainly he seems to me not only to hold
as literal truth that 'Paradisus est locus corporeus', which
is the matter before him, but to see little difficulty, supposing (which of course he does not grant) that the literal

sense was not historic, or was doubtful, in interpreting the whole account spiritually or even figuratively. Therefore, if the case occurred of small inaccuracies of fact in Scripture history, instead of countenancing me in saying that, in matters which did not infringe upon faith and morals, such apparent error was of no serious consequence, I grant that he would have preferred, (and with St Augustine,) to interpret a passage, so characterised, in a spiritual sense, or according to some other secondary sense, which he thinks it possible to give to Scripture. Here it is, I grant, that I should not have his countenance; he would not indeed forbid me to say that a statement was *literally* inaccurate, but he would rather wish me to find some interpretation for it which would give it an edifying sense. Thus St Augustine, when questioned as to Jacob's conduct towards his father and brother, appeals from that grave question to its typical and evangelical meaning: 'Non est mendacium, sed mysterium'.

What makes me so conclude is a passage in his Quæst. iii de Potentia.[1] He there speaks of the danger, 'ne aliquis ita Scripturam ad unum sensum cogere velit, quod alios sensus, qui in se veritatem continent, et possunt, salvâ circumstantia litteræ, Scripturæ aptari, penitus excludantur.'[2] Then he says that the dignity of Scripture requires many senses under one letter. He concludes by saying, 'Omnis veritas, quæ, salvâ litteræ circumstantia, potest divinæ Scripturæ aptari, *est ejus sensus*'.[3]

---

[1] Sic; it is actually q. 4, art. 1, corpus.

[2] 'Lest anyone might wish to restrict Scripture to one sense, in such a way as entirely to exclude other senses which contain truth and can, without violence to the context, be made to fit Scripture'.

[3] 'Every truth which, without violence to the context, can be made to fit Holy Scripture *is its sense*'.

§ 35.

Restrictions upon Inspiration

St Augustine and St Thomas are such great names in
the Church that he must be a bold Catholic, who, knowing
what they are, should contradict them. But they cannot
rightly be taken instead of *her* Voice.[1] There are numbers
of good Catholics who never heard of them, and many
of these learned and accomplished in their respective ways
and callings, and earnestly desirous to remain in the faith
and fear of Holy Church. And, as I would not dare to treat
the above-mentioned Fathers with disrespect, much less
should I dare to speak against the teaching of the Church
herself; and when the Church has distinctly taught us in
two Ecumenical Councils, once and again, at the interval
of three hundred years, and in very different conditions of
human society, that the divine inspiration of Scripture is
to be assigned especially *rebus fidei et morum*, it shocks me
to find a Catholic Professor asserting that such a dogmatic
decision is what he calls a *restriction*; a charge as inconsistent with good logic as with tenderness towards a
decision of the Church. Of course I have no intention of
complaining of his adding to the Church's decision the
conclusions of theology or the anticipations of devotion,
but her person (if I may so speak of the Church) is sacred;
and she has reasons for all she does, and all she does not do.
We should never forget who is minister and who is Lord.

So much for (what I fear I must call) the impropriety of
the word 'restriction' when applied to a literal quotation
of mine from the definitions of two Ecumenical Councils.
Now for its failure in logic.

The Professor affirms, speaking (as I understand him)
of what he seems to consider in this case not more than an

[1] 'Her voice': C, 'the Church'.

hypothesis, namely,[1] the 'clause' *in rebus fidei et morum*, that it is 'a restricting clause', and that 'the Catholic dogma is adequately and accurately expressed only by *eliminating* that clause'. Eliminating! He cannot be using so great a word with reference to any mere statement of mine; it fits on to nothing short of the dogmatic utterances of the two Ecumenical Councils. He has said nothing in order to guard against this natural conclusion, and as if to make it the clearer, he contrasts it with my own words, to the effect that 'sacred Scripture is inspired *throughout*'.

But I would observe, that, easy as it is to speak against 'restrictions' being placed on the gift of inspiration, those who would impute the blame, whether to the Church or to me, are also incurring it themselves. For instance, if Scripture is the Word of God (as in a true sense it is), and inspiration is (in the Professor's sense) *throughout* it, it cannot but be *verbally* inspired; but the prevalent opinion now is that this is not the case. How is this not putting a restriction upon inspiration? How is it *thorough*, if the *language* of Scripture is not included in it? Yet the Professor, who is so disturbed at my appealing to the dogmatic force of *'fides et mores'*, has no scruple whatever in depriving inspiration of its action upon the language of the writers of Scripture. He ventures to say, in spite of the dissent of great Fathers, that 'God in most cases *did* leave the choice of the words to the writer'; and he speaks of the opinion, that the Holy Spirit dictated the sacred books word for word, as having been 'held by a few, and now generally and justly rejected'. Thus he speaks. It seems that he may say *without* Ecumenical Councils what another may not say *with* them.

Nor is this the only 'restriction' which he allows upon the inspiration of Scripture. He does not quite commit

[1] 'What . . . namely': not in C.

himself to it as an opinion, but he does not quarrel with those who hold it, viz., that inspiration goes as far as, but not further than, the *'res et sententias'* of Scripture, beyond which, it seems, the inspiration does not reach; he calls for no 'eliminating' process here.

But something more has to be said still on the Professor's mode of arguing. Nothing is more difficult in controversy than the skilful use of metaphors. A metaphor has a dozen aspects, and, unless we look sharp, we shall be slain by the rebound of one or other of our deductions from them. Now if there be an idea intimately connected or present to us when in theology[1] we speak of a *'word'*, it is that of a personal agent, from whom the word proceeds. It is an effect which does not exist without a cause. It must have a speaker or writer, and but one such. In this[2] case one effect cannot have two causes. If two are ascribed to it, one or other must be ascribed metaphorically. We cannot refer it to each of two causes at one time in its full sense. But the Professor takes it in its highest sense, as the Word of God, when he would prove that Scripture had no imperfections in it; yet when he would relieve himself of the difficulties, and account for defects, of language, then it is the word of man. Of course the inspiration of Scripture is from above; but what I want to be told is, are we to consider a book of Scripture, whether written or spoken, literally the Word of God or literally the word of man?

§ 36.

Plenary as well as Present Inspiration[3]

But it may be objected, in answer to what I have been

[1] 'In theology': not in C.
[2] 'In this case': C, 'Here'.
[3] C, *'Plenary and Permanent Inspiration'*.

saying in explanation of 'restriction', that the Council of the Vatican, treating of inspiration, has added to the dogma of Trent a clause which destroys the distinction which I have been making as to the special object with reference to which the sacred writers were endowed with the gift. For the Vatican Council has dogmatically determined the books of holy Scripture, 'libros *integros cum omnibus suis partibus,* inspiratos esse'; and if the whole of Scripture in all its parts is inspired, how can inspiration be restricted to the matters of faith and morals? Yet I conceive this difficulty admits of an easy reply.

Certainly I have no wish to explain away the words of the Council; but is there no distinction between a gift itself, and the purpose for which it was made, and the use to which it is to be applied? We meet with this[1] distinction every day. Might not a benefactor leave a legacy to the whole of a large family of children, one and all, yet under the condition that it was expended solely on their education? And so Scripture is inspired in its length and breadth, and is brought into the compass of one volume by virtue of this supernatural bond; whenever, wherever, and by whomsoever written, it is all inspired: still we may ask the question, In what respect, and for what purpose?

When we speak of the Bible in its length and breadth, we speak of it quantitatively; but this does not interfere with our viewing it in relation to the character, or what may be called the quality, of the inspiration. According to the two Councils, Scripture is inspired as being the work of inspired men, the subject of faith and morals being the occupation or mission assigned to them and their writings, and inspiration being the efficient cause of their teaching.

Each of these truths is independent of, is consistent with, each. The plenary extent of inspiration, and the definite

[1] C, 'the'.

object of it, neither of these can interfere, neither can be confused, with the other. Because a cup is full, that does enable us to determine what is the nature and the effects of the liquor with which it is filled; whether, for instance, it is nutritive or medicinal or merely restorative;[1] and so, though Scripture be plenarily inspired, it is a question still, for what purposes, and in what way.[2]

In a word, Inspiration of Scripture in omnibus *suis partibus* is one thing; in omnibus *rebus* is another.

It may be asked how inspiration could be given to the Sacred Writers for faith and morals, whereas they were not always writing, and when they did write, needed not be writing on religious and ethical subjects. Thus St Paul, when he wrote about his *penula*, was he not in possession of a divine gift which on that occasion he could not use? But we see instances of this every day. A man may be strong without opportunity of using his strength, and a man may have a good memory or be a good linguist though he exercises his gift only now and then; and so a passage of Scripture may have spiritual meanings, as St Thomas would hold, and may avail for edification with a force which an uninspired writing has not, though the literal sense may refer to matters purely secular and human, as the passage in John ii, 10, which I have quoted in my Article.

§ 37.

Inspiration as Co-ordinate with Error.

There is one subject more, on which it may be expedient to dwell for a few minutes.

---

[1] C, 'refreshing'.
[2] 'and in what way': not in C.

The Professor insists on its being a conclusion theologically certain that everything that is to be found in the Sacred Writers is literally the Word of God; and in consequence he would imply that I, by questioning whether some words in Scripture may not come from the writers themselves mainly, have committed the serious act of rejecting a theological truth. Now, of course it is indisputable that a proposition, which is the immediate consequence of a truth of Revelation, is itself a certain truth. Certainly; but it is a further question whether this or that conclusion is an instance of such a real demonstration. This indeed I say frankly, that, if my certainties depended on the Professor's syllogisms, I should have small chance of making a decent show of theological certainties.

For instance, in the present question, he has proved just the contrary to what he meant to prove, as can easily be shown. He had to prove that it is theologically certain that the whole of Scripture, whatever is contained in it, is the Word of God, and this is how he does it. He says, 'It is as absurd to say that a man could commit sin under the *impulse* of the Holy Ghost, as to say that the Sacred Writers could write error under the inspiration of the Holy Ghost.' Why does he change 'impulse' into 'inspiration' in the second clause of his sentence? Who ever fancied that the *impulse* of the Holy Spirit might cause error? Who will deny that the impulse of the Holy Spirit would certainly be accorded to an Apostle or Prophet to hinder, even in a statement of fact, any serious error? If the Holy Spirit does not hinder varieties and errors in transcribers of Scripture which damage the perfection of His work, why should He hinder small errors (on the hypothesis that such there are) of the original writers? Is not He, with the Church co-operating, sufficient for a Guardian?

But this is not all. He says that error cannot co-exist with inspiration, more than sin with grace; but grace *can* co-exist with sin. His parallel just turns against him. Good Christians are each 'the Temple of God', 'partakers of the Divine Nature', nay 'gods', and they are said 'portare Deum in corpore suo'; and priests, I consider, have not less holiness than others; yet every priest in his daily Mass asks pardon 'pro innumerabilibus peccatis et offensionibus et negligentiis meis'. Grace brings a soul nearer to God than inspiration, for Balaam and Caiphas were inspired; yet the Professor tells us that, though sin is possible in spite of grace, error is impossible because of inspiration.[1]

Thus I answer the special remarks made by my Critic[2] on my February Article; should other objections be urged against it, I trust they would be found to admit of as direct an explanation.

J. H. N.

May, 1884.

[1] C added: 'I have not dared to speak against any decision of the great doctors St Augustine and St Thomas, but I feel it sad indeed that from a Professor in a School of Theology, so widely known and so time-honoured, they should sustain the indignity of so unsatisfactory an advocacy, and that too directed against one whose ecclesiastical station might have advantageously suggested criticism in a milder tone.'

[2] 'My Critic': C, 'Professor Healy'.